Discussing Crime

Learning Resource Centre

Email: LRC@swindon.ac.uk   Tel: (01793) 491⁵

Independence Educational Publishers

First published by Independence Educational Publishers

The Studio, High Green

Great Shelford

Cambridge CB22 5EG

England

© Independence 2016

ISBN-13: 9781861687319

Printed in Great Britain
Zenith Print Group

Contents

Introduction

Discussing Crime is Volume 295 in the **ISSUES** series. The aim of the series is to offer current, diverse information about important issues in our world, from a UK perspective.

ABOUT DISCUSSING CRIME

Figures from the Office of National Statistics revealed that there were 6.8 million incidents of crime against households and resident adults for the year ending March 2015. This book explores which crimes are increasing and which are falling. It also considers issues such as crime and mental health, knife crime in the UK and the influence of social media on crime. The justice system is also explored, paying particular attention to the experiences of young people.

OUR SOURCES

Titles in the **ISSUES** series are designed to function as educational resource books, providing a balanced overview of a specific subject.

The information in our books is comprised of facts, articles and opinions from many different sources, including:

⇨ Newspaper reports and opinion pieces

⇨ Website factsheets

⇨ Magazine and journal articles

⇨ Statistics and surveys

⇨ Government reports

⇨ Literature from special interest groups

A NOTE ON CRITICAL EVALUATION

Because the information reprinted here is from a number of different sources, readers should bear in mind the origin of the text and whether the source is likely to have a particular bias when presenting information (or when conducting their research). It is hoped that, as you read about the many aspects of the issues explored in this book, you will critically evaluate the information presented.

It is important that you decide whether you are being presented with facts or opinions. Does the writer give a biased or unbiased report? If an opinion is being expressed, do you agree with the writer? Is there potential bias to the 'facts' or statistics behind an article?

ASSIGNMENTS

In the back of this book, you will find a selection of assignments designed to help you engage with the articles you have been reading and to explore your own opinions. Some tasks will take longer than others and there is a mixture of design, writing and research-based activities that you can complete alone or in a group.

FURTHER RESEARCH

At the end of each article we have listed its source and a website that you can visit if you would like to conduct your own research. Please remember to critically evaluate any sources that you consult and consider whether the information you are viewing is accurate and unbiased.

Useful weblinks

www.amnesty.org.uk

www.beyondyouthcustody.net

www.bsa.natcen.ac.uk

www.cardiff.ac.uk

www.childrenssociety.org.uk

www.clinks.org

www.theconversation.com

www.cycj.org.uk

www.edp24.co.uk

www.theguardian.com

www.mdx.ac.uk

www.ons.gov.uk

Politics.co.uk

www.portsmouth.co.uk

www.prisonreformtrust.org.uk

www.sussex.police.uk

www.telegraph.co.uk

www.ucl.ac.uk

www.vice.com

www.victimsupport.org.uk

Crime in England and Wales, year ending March 2015

⇨ Latest figures from the Crime Survey for England and Wales (CSEW) showed that, for the offences it covers, there were an estimated 6.8 million incidents of crime against households and resident adults (aged 16 and over). This is a 7% decrease compared with the previous year's survey, and the lowest estimate since the CSEW began in 1981.

⇨ The decrease in all CSEW crime was driven by a reduction in the all theft offences category (down 8%). Within this group there were falls in the sub-categories of theft from the person (down 21%) and other theft of personal property (down 22%). However, there was no significant change in other sub-categories such as domestic burglary and vehicle-related theft.

⇨ In contrast to the CSEW, there was a 3% increase in police recorded crime compared with the previous year, with 3.8 million offences recorded in the year ending March 2015.

⇨ The rise in the police figures was driven by increases in violence against the person offences (up by 23% compared with the previous year). However, this increase is thought to reflect changes in recording practices rather than a rise in violent crime. The CSEW estimate for violent crime showed no change compared with the previous year's survey, following decreases over the past four years.

⇨ Offences involving knives and sharp instruments increased by 2% in the year ending March 2015. This small rise masked more significant changes at offence level with an increase in assaults (up 13%, from 11,911 to 13,488) and a decrease in robberies (down 14%, from 11,927 to 10,270). In addition, the related category of weapon possession offences also rose by 10% (from 9,050 to 9,951). Such serious offences are not thought to be prone to changes in recording practice.

⇨ Sexual offences recorded by the police rose by 37% with the numbers of rapes (29,265) and other sexual offences (58,954) being at the highest level since the introduction of the National Crime Recording Standard in 2002/03. As well as improvements in recording, this is also thought to reflect a greater willingness of victims to come forward to report such crimes. In contrast, the latest estimate from the CSEW showed no significant change in the proportion of adults aged 16–59 who reported being a victim of a sexual assault (including attempted assaults) in the last year (1.7%).

⇨ While other acquisitive crimes recorded by the police continued to decline there was an increase in the volume of fraud offences recorded by Action Fraud (up 9%) largely driven by increases in non-investment fraud (up 15%) – a category which includes frauds related to online shopping and computer software services. This is the first time a year-on-year comparison can be made on a like-for-like basis. It is difficult to know whether this means actual levels of fraud rose or simply that a greater proportion of victims reported to Action Fraud. However, other sources also show year-on-year increases, including data supplied to the National Fraud Investigation Bureau from industry sources (up 17%).

16 July 2015

⇨ The above information is reprinted with kind permission from the Office for National Statistics. Please visit www.ons.gov.uk for further information.

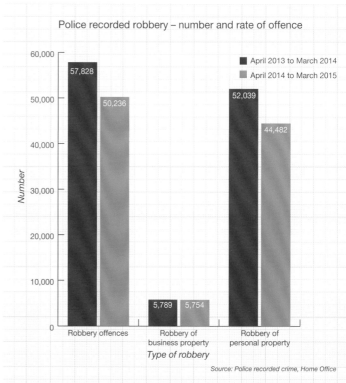

Police recorded robbery – number and rate of offence

- April 2013 to March 2014
- April 2014 to March 2015

Robbery offences: 57,828 / 50,236
Robbery of business property: 5,789 / 5,754
Robbery of personal property: 52,039 / 44,482

Number

Type of robbery

Source: Police recorded crime, Home Office

Which crimes are going up and which are falling?

Why are some crimes in the region falling, while others are on the rise? David Powles investigates.

The year is 2003 and Norfolk Police is being swamped by vehicle-related crime.

In the 12 months previously their figures show they dealt with 11,440 such offences.

That is about one-sixth of all recorded crime in the county, hours of manpower and lots of pain and disruption for the victims.

Fast-forward 11 years and that figure reads very differently.

While overall crime has fallen, vehicle-related offences have plummeted – there were 2,334 in the whole of 2014. It is the same in Suffolk, where vehicle crime fell from 7,152 to 3,186.

This is just one area where, according to the statistics, certain crimes are being driven out of our communities.

Yet our study of recorded police statistics for the past 11 years show this is not the case for all offences. In Norfolk, Suffolk and Cambridgeshire, shoplifting, drug offences and violence have bucked the trend.

Crime experts question whether the statistics can be trusted.

There are two main ways crime is assessed in Britain – using figures provided by police forces and the Crime Survey for England and Wales.

There have been concerns about the reliability of those issued by forces and last year the UK Statistics Authority withdrew their gold standard status after hearing evidence of forces under-recording.

Dr Nic Groombridge, criminologist from St Mary's University at Twickenham, believed they could still be a useful tool to track emerging trends.

He said: "There is a vast amount of crime that isn't picked up by police records, the crime survey or other organisations. Some crimes aren't reported, sometimes people don't even know they've been a victim of crime.

"But these figures are a good indication of the reasons people have for calling the police."

So why have some risen, while others fall?

As far as vehicle crime is concerned technology has played a big part.

Dr Groombridge said: "This is one we can be fairly confident about. The reduction is largely down to car manufacturers suddenly realising that security was a factor as to why people brought cars and improving security measures."

The same can be said for burglary and cycle theft. There were 3,820 house burglaries in Norfolk in 2003, compared to 1,311 last year. In Suffolk they fell from 2,284 to 1,391.

Even though cycling has become increasingly popular in recent years, crime prevention has improved and the figures have remained relatively static.

Elsewhere, theft in Norfolk fell from 11,987 to 5,781 and Suffolk from 6,224 to 4,794 and robbery from 579 to 199 in Norfolk and 249 to 164 in Suffolk. The picture was similar in Cambridgeshire.

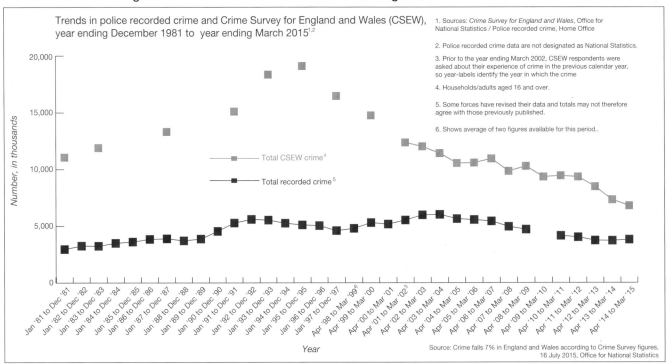

Trends in police recorded crime and Crime Survey for England and Wales (CSEW), year ending December 1981 to year ending March 2015[1,2]

1. Sources: *Crime Survey for England and Wales*, Office for National Statistics / Police recorded crime, Home Office

2. Police recorded crime data are not designated as National Statistics.

3. Prior to the year ending March 2002, CSEW respondents were asked about their experience of crime in the previous calendar year, so year-labels identify the year in which the crime

4. Households/adults aged 16 and over.

5. Some forces have revised their data and totals may not therefore agree with those previously published.

6. Shows average of two figures available for this period..

Source: Crime falls 7% in England and Wales according to Crime Survey figures, 16 July 2015, Office for National Statistics

Experts said crime was moving behind closed doors.

Dr Groombridge added: "There is a school of thought that people who were previously out on the streets offending, committing burglaries and robberies, are now back at home doing it in the cyber world on games such as *Gran Theft Auto*.

"But what we are seeing is an increase in cyber offences. We've moved towards a cashless society which makes one type of crime less likely, but opens a new door."

And what of those crimes that are on the rise? In 12 years, shoplifting in Norfolk has risen slightly from 3,730 to 3,857, but there was a sharp spike in 2007, 2009 and 2011. In Essex the figures rose from 3,289 to 3,663.

That was when the recession hit hard and people were more likely to take desperate measures.

Violence offences, with or without injury, rose slightly in all counties, while there was also a rise in sex offences from 729 to 1,300 in Norfolk and 634 in 2003 to 1,028 in Suffolk.

Dr Groombridge said: "Generally police will say these figures have risen because reporting has gone up."

Historic sex offences have featured heavily in the public eye in recent years and this will have impacted the figures.

Norfolk Police also dealt with many more drugs offences in 2014, rising from 1,392 to 2,579, while Suffolk drug offences also rose, but Dr Groombridge claimed this may be a case of police putting more priority on to it.

In general, official crime has fallen dramatically for all three of our forces, and Dr Groombridge said: "I'm fairly confident that crime is going down. I suspect however that a lot of people will think that crime is not going down as there is always a problem of perception."

What now for crime?

Many experts in criminology share the view that cyber-related crime will become more common place.

One reason for this, according to Dr Groombridge, is because many of these crimes currently go unreported. Eventually the statistics will catch up with the true picture.

Meanwhile, as anti-crime technology improves, this will have an impact. Dr Groombridge said: "In terms of shoplifting we are still waiting for technology to catch up. When they put tracking devices on items such as bottles of whisky or clothes it prevented people from stealing them. But the smaller items don't currently have them. There may come a time when they will.

"The reason mobiles are so popular to steal is that they are mobile. They can be taken, then used. There will come a time when technology makes it harder to make use of a stolen mobile."

Dr Groombridge believes there is a danger that technology can take things too far.

He explained: "There is an enormous amount we can do to drive down crime completely if you are really hell-bent, but would we want to live in a society like that?

"One of the downsides of freedom is you have to have some crime.

"I am concerned by the things we have done in terms of some of the smaller crimes, those police previously may have turned a blind eye to.

"If everything is monitored on speed cameras and CCTV you are going to get more crimes and going to need more jails. At a low level we are seeing lots of things criminalised to some level, e.g. fines for parking.

"If you say you want to completely eradicate crime you have to be careful as you may lose a lot of freedom as well."

11 May 2015

⇨ The above information is reprinted with kind permission from the *Eastern Daily Press*. Please visit www.edp24. co.uk for further information.

The mental health needs of gang – affiliated young people

A briefing produced as part of the Ending Gang and Youth Violence programme.

Executive summary

⇨ Research is beginning to expose the high burden of mental illness faced by young people involved with gangs. Gang members are at increased risk of a range of mental health conditions including conduct disorder, antisocial personality disorder, anxiety, psychosis and drug and alcohol dependence.

⇨ The links between gang affiliation and poor mental health can operate in both directions. Poor mental wellbeing can draw young people to gangs while gang involvement can negatively impact on an individual's mental health.

⇨ Violence is an inherent part of gang culture and gang members are at increased risk of involvement in violence as both perpetrators and victims. Long-term exposure to violence is associated with psychological problems including depression, conduct disorders and post-traumatic stress disorder.

⇨ Poor mental health and gang affiliation share many common risk factors, often relating to young people's early life experiences and the environments in which they grow up. The more risk factors young people are exposed to the greater their vulnerability to negative outcomes.

⇨ Girls involved with gangs can be particularly vulnerable to mental health problems resulting from sexual and intimate partner violence.

⇨ Preventing the development of risk factors and promoting mental wellbeing in young people requires a life course approach that supports parents and families and encourages healthy development from the very earliest stages of life.

⇨ Programmes such as home visiting, parenting programmes, preschool programmes and school-based social and emotional development programmes can protect children from the risk factors for gang involvement and poor mental health, including parental stress, exposure to violence and behavioural problems.

⇨ Evidence-based, relevant, accessible and non-stigmatising community interventions should be available in gang-affected areas to promote health and emotional wellbeing, support recovery from mental illness and help young people move away from harmful gang-related activities

⇨ Gang-affiliated young people may experience particular barriers to engaging with mental health and other services. Novel approaches are required, including the provision of holistic support in young peoples' own environments and the use of key workers or mentors who are able to build trusting relationships with young people involved with gangs.

⇨ Effectively addressing the relationships between gang affiliation and poor mental health requires a strong, collaborative approach that co-ordinates services across a wide range of organisations. Health services, local authorities, schools, criminal justice agencies and communities all have an important role to play in promoting healthy social and emotional development in children and young people and ensuring vulnerable young people affected by gangs and poor mental health receive the support they require.

27 January 2015

⇨ The above information is reprinted with kind permission from Public Health England. Please visit www.gov.uk for further information.

Knife crime in England and Wales up for first time in four years

ONS reveals 2% rise in total knife crime offences in year to March as 'two strikes and you're out' jail sentence for possession comes into force.

By Alan Travis

Knife crime has increased in England and Wales for the first time in four years, with the number of assaults with blades rising 13%, according to the latest set of police recorded crime figures.

The Office for National Statistics said the 2% rise in all knife crime offences in the 12 months to March marked the end of a downward trend in the previous four years but the total remained more than 50% below its peak six years ago.

The increase to 26,370 offences was announced ahead of a new 'two strikes and you're out' mandatory prison sentence for repeated possession of a knife or blade coming into effect on Friday. More than 1,000 extra offenders are expected to be jailed every year under the measure.

John Flatley, head of crime statistics at the ONS, said the rise in knife crime was real and unlikely to be due to changes in recording practices. He said: "We have seen year-on-year reductions over the last four or five years. This year it has turned slightly. It is a reversal of what we have seen in recent years."

The quarterly crime figures also show an increase in fraud, particularly online fraud, with online shopping and computer software scams reported to the police rising by 15% over the past year.

Meanwhile, Home Office figures show that the number of police officers has fallen by a further 1,091 over the past year to 126,818. The number of operational frontline officers fell to 113,134 at the end of March, 12,000 fewer than in 2010 as a result of the austerity budget cuts.

The increase in knife crime is one factor fuelling a 3% increase in the police recorded crime figures. The ONS said this rise to 3.8 million offences was driven by a 23% increase in offences involving violence against the person, although "this increase is thought to reflect changes in recording practices rather than a rise in violent crime".

The official statisticians also point to a 7% fall in the figures from the official crime survey of England and Wales, which estimates there were 6.8 million incidents – the lowest level since the survey began in 1981.

The ONS said that the 7% fall in the crime survey estimate included a 21% fall in thefts from the person and a 22% drop in thefts of other personal property.

The ONS also said the overall 2% rise in knife crime recorded by the police masked more significant changes in the detail, with a 13% increase in assaults involving a knife, and a 10% rise in knife possession offences. However, robberies at knifepoint fell by 14%.

The official police recorded crime figures also show an apparently startling 37% increase in sexual offences, including rapes. The number of rapes reported to the police was 29,265 – the highest level since new recording standards were introduced 12 years ago.

But the ONS said the surge was due to a greater willingness of victims to come forward and report such crimes and improvements in police recording rather than an increase in sexual attacks. It said the official crime survey showed no significant change in the proportion of adults who reported being a victim of a sexual assault last year.

The underlying theme of the figures – that England and Wales continues to become a safer country – is underlined by the homicide rate. The police recorded 534 murders in the 12 months to March – only one more than in the previous year – and close to the lowest level since 1978 when 532 people were murdered.

The annual murder rate for England and Wales stood at more than 800 a year in the early years of the 21st century but over the past decade has fallen while the population has continued to grow.

Home Office minister Mike Penning said the 7% fall in crime as measured by the official crime survey was "good news for a safer England and Wales". He said the action taken by the Home Secretary to improve the quality of police crime recording was already leading to improvements and more victims of sexual offences and domestic abuse were coming forward.

He added that while the figures also showed the size of the police workforce had reduced, the rate of decline was slowing and 13 forces had increased their police officer numbers in the last year.

The crime charity Victim Support said: "After years of success in driving knife crime down, this rise is a worrying development and efforts to educate people about the dangers of carrying knives must be stepped up."

Irene Curtis, president of the Police Superintendents' Association, said the figures showed it was clear that policing was going to have to change significantly, with 17,000 fewer officers than five years ago and certain types of crime rising and further budget cuts on the way.

16 July 2015

⇨ The above information is reprinted with kind permission from *The Guardian*. Please visit www.theguardian.com for further information.

Buying and carrying knives: the law

The laws about buying and carrying a knife depend on the type of knife, your age and your circumstances.

Basic laws on knives

It is illegal to:

⇨ sell a knife of any kind to anyone under 18 years old (16- to 18-year-olds in Scotland can buy cutlery and kitchen knives)

⇨ carry a knife in public without good reason – unless it's a knife with a folding blade three inches long (7.62 cm) or less, e.g. a Swiss Army knife

⇨ carry, buy or sell any type of banned knife

⇨ use any knife in a threatening way (even a legal knife, such as a Swiss Army knife)

Lock knives (knives with blades that can be locked when unfolded) are not folding knives, and are illegal to carry in public without good reason.

The maximum penalty for an adult carrying a knife is four years in prison and a fine of £5,000.

Good reasons for carrying a knife

Examples of good reasons to carry a knife in public can include:

⇨ taking knives you use at work to and from work

⇨ taking knives to a gallery or museum to be exhibited

⇨ the knife is going to be used for theatre, film, television, historical reenactment or religious purposes, e.g. the kirpan some Sikhs carry

A court will decide if you've got a good reason to carry a knife if you're charged with carrying it illegally.

Banned knives

There is a ban on the sale of some knives:

⇨ flick knives (also called 'switchblades' or 'automatic knives') – where the blade is hidden inside the handle and shoots out when a button is pressed

⇨ butterfly knives – where the blade is hidden inside a handle that splits in two around it, like wings; the handles swing around the blade to open or close it

⇨ disguised knives, e.g. where the blade is hidden inside a belt buckle or fake mobile phone

⇨ gravity knives

⇨ sword-sticks

⇨ samurai swords (with some exceptions, including antiques and swords made to traditional methods before 1954)

⇨ hand or foot-claws

⇨ push daggers

⇨ hollow kubotan (cylinder-shaped keychain) holding spikes

⇨ shuriken (also known as 'death stars' or 'throwing stars')

⇨ kusari-gama (sickle attached to a rope, cord or wire)

⇨ kyoketsu-shoge (hook-knife attached to a rope, cord or wire)

⇨ kusari (weight attached to a rope, cord or wire).

This is not a complete list of banned knives. Contact your local police to check if a knife is illegal.

22 January 2015

⇨ The above information is reprinted with kind permission from GOV.UK.

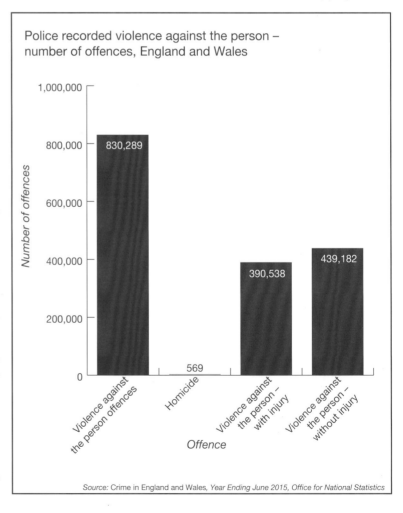

Police recorded violence against the person – number of offences, England and Wales

Number of offences

- Violence against the person offences: 830,289
- Homicide: 569
- Violence against the person – with injury: 390,538
- Violence against the person – without injury: 439,182

Offence

Source: Crime in England and Wales, Year Ending June 2015, Office for National Statistics

Half of young offenders are themselves victims, finds new study

Half of 11- 17-year-olds in the hands of Youth Offending Services have themselves been the victim of abuse, violence, crime or other traumatic experiences, finds a new report by Middlesex University. Most of these have emotional and mental health needs that are linked to these experiences.

The research, conducted by Middlesex University for the Mayor's Office for Policing And Crime (MOPAC), is intended to inform the development of support services for young people who have offended but have themselves been a victim of crime, abuse and violence.

"Young people are often reluctant to take up the offer of support with mental health problems, not least because of the stigma that comes with this"

Signs or disclosure of past traumatic experiences may only become apparent after an offender has been in the system for a period of time. The report also calls for all Youth Offending Services to review screening processes for emotional and mental health distress, and provide training in recognising signs and vulnerability.

The report's lead author, Middlesex University Associate Professor in Criminology David Porteous, said: "Young people are often reluctant to take up the offer of support with mental health problems, not least because of the stigma that comes with this. Within Youth Offending Services, building trusting relationships is an essential first step.

"At a broader level we need to reflect on the implications of the overlap between offending and victimisation, to understand that an offender and victim can be the same person but in a different time and place, and that the contexts in which crime tends to be concentrated are as much part of the problem as the particular individuals involved."

Stephen Greenhalgh, Deputy Mayor for Policing and Crime, said: "This new report from Middlesex University reveals fresh evidence of the catastrophic and enduring effect that crime can have on the life of a young person.

I am determined that do more to break the vicious cycle of violence. This research provides valuable new insights on how to prevent youth offending and reduce re-offending. I am delighted that MOPAC are sharing it with other practitioners around the country by publishing it on our website."

"We need to reflect on the implications of the overlap between offending and victimisation, to understand that an offender and victim can be the same person but in a different time and place"

The Mayor's Office has secured £400,000 from the Ministry of Justice Victim's Fund to develop new services for these young people and the report outlines alternative ways in which this money might be put to use. Domestic and street violence, sexual abuse, rape, bereavement and bullying are all traumas identified in the report which can have negative effects on youngsters.

29 May 2015

⇨ The above information is reprinted with kind permission from Middlesex University London. Please visit www.mdx.ac.uk for further information.

Older teenagers in London "living in fear"

Tens of thousands of older teenagers in London feel unsafe in the city – and thousands run away from home every year, according to new research by The Children's Society.

The charity highlighted the figures as it prepares to unveil a network of services across the capital to tackle the risks facing the city's vulnerable young people.

In a survey by the charity, whose new London hub will launch on 2 July, a third of 16- and 17-year-olds told The Children's Society they feel unsafe in common public areas like bus stations, train stations, or car parks – that's equivalent to 61,000 young people across the city.

Almost one in five (19%) reported feeling unsafe in youth or after-school clubs. And 7% say they even feel unsafe in their own home – twice the level of the rest of the country.

Constant access to the Internet and social media is creating new pressures and risks, with one in eight (12%) now reporting that they do not feel safe online.

It is clear from the figures – from a UK-wide survey carried out for The Children's Society by Opinium – that 16- and 17-year-olds feel under pressure to do a range of things they might not freely choose to do. About one in seven respondents (13%) said they had found themselves under pressure to spend time with people they did not feel comfortable with. And one in ten said they felt pressurised to have sex.

At the same time, a worryingly low proportion of teenagers say they would choose to go to the authorities for help if one of their friends got into trouble. Only 16% said they would go to a professional if a friend was experiencing exploitation. Even fewer would go to authorities for help if their friend was in a damaging relationship (6%) or had run away from home (11%).

Separate research by The Children's Society, based on Freedom of Information requests submitted to London local authorities, shows at least 2,000 young people went missing from home across 20 London boroughs last year. Too few of them are getting an independent return interview – meaning they may be left without follow-up support and placed at greater risk.

All the findings have been published in a new report, *Streets of London: Keeping Adolescents Safe*.

Far from being streetwise and able to protect themselves, as they are sometimes characterised, older teens are more likely to be victims of crime and are particularly vulnerable to abuse and neglect.

But teenagers suffering abuse and neglect are being overlooked by children's services because they are deemed older and more resilient – even when they lack the financial independence to remove themselves from harmful situations.

The Children's Society's network of projects will bring together the expertise of practitioners across the capital to reach out to young people facing issues such as sexual exploitation, trafficking, destitution and going missing from home. It will also advocate for some of the most vulnerable young people living in the city, such as refugees and migrants and young people who are disabled.

The work to support vulnerable teenagers is being supported by a campaign launching on 26 June, Seriously Awkward, asking the Government to do more to protect vulnerable 16- and 17-year-olds from harm, abuse and neglect.

Sherry Peck, Area Director for The Children's Society in London, said: "Too many older teenagers in London are living in fear for their safety and we need to challenge the idea that 16- and 17-year-olds don't require as much protection as younger children. In fact they are more likely to find themselves in risky situations, without the life experience to deal with them, and many vulnerable young people are in desperate need of help.

'The Children's Society's network of services across the capital will be fully focused on providing support to transform the lives of vulnerable teenagers who run away from home, or who are at risk of sexual exploitation or mental illness. We will work with local authorities to achieve this but we also need Government to take action to make sure that older teenagers get the legal protection they deserve."

In London...

⇨ 518,892 children live in poverty – 74% of whose parents are in work

⇨ More than one in ten children and young people have a clinically significant mental health condition.

⇨ An estimated 3,420 children aged 16 and 17 asked their local authority for help last year because they were at risk of becoming homeless.

⇨ The number of children subject to a Child Protection Plan has increased by 40% in the last decade.

⇨ Young people in the most deprived areas are six times more likely to be the victims of crime than those living in the wealthiest areas.

25 June 2015

⇨ The above information is reprinted with kind permission from The Children's Society. Please visit www.childrenssociety.org.uk for further information.

Suffering in silence

Children and unreported crime.

Executive summary

This report presents the findings of a Scoping Inquiry into the hidden victimisation of children and young people, undertaken on behalf of the All Party Parliamentary Group (APPG) for Victims and Witnesses of Crime. The inquiry was commissioned in response to findings from the most recent Crime Survey for England and Wales which indicates that less than one-fifth of children and young people who experience theft or violent crime report this to the police. The charity Victim Support, who provides the secretariat to the APPG, undertook research for the Inquiry in partnership with the University of Bedfordshire. Evidence was gathered in four ways:

⇨ a short review of existing literature;

⇨ an analysis of relevant data sources including the Crime Survey for England and Wales;

⇨ a rapid call for evidence from charities, service providers, statutory bodies and campaigners; and

⇨ three focus groups with children and young people.

Findings

1. Children and young people experience much higher rates of crime than police data suggests

⇨ Research shows significant levels of crime and victimisation amongst children and young people. Approximately one-third of 11– 17-year-olds, for example, report experiencing physical violence within the last year. One-quarter of 11- 24-year-olds say they experienced some form of abuse or neglect during childhood.

⇨ Evidence indicates that children and young people are at higher risk than adults of experiencing certain forms of crime. Females aged 16 to 19 years, for example, are the age group at highest risk of being a victim of a sexual offence.

⇨ Existing vulnerabilities, such as a long-standing illness or disability, appear to significantly compound children and young people's vulnerability to crime.

⇨ The majority of crimes against children and young people are not reported to the police. Only 13% of violent offences and 15% of thefts are reported by young victims. Similarly, retrospectiveaccounts of childhood sexual abuse show only 5–13% of victims reported this to an adult at the time.

⇨ Whilst existing data offers pertinent insights, determining accurate prevalence levels of children and young people's victimisation remains challenging due to variable approaches to collecting and categorising data.

2. Children and young people don't always know what constitutes crime and how to report this

⇨ Many children and young people do not realise that what they have experienced constitutes a crime or other form of victimisation requiring support and redress. This is particularly true where forms of criminal behaviour have been normalised within a peer group or a community, or when grooming by another individual is a factor.

⇨ Children and young people don't always know how to report experiences of victimisation. Teachers are the professionals they are most likely to tell but they, and other professionals, often lack confidence about how to recognise and respond to reports of children's victimisation.

3. The context in which victimisation occurs affects the likelihood of reporting

⇨ The fact that much of children and young people's victimisation occurs in contexts, such as school, where perpetrators are known to the victim significantly reduces the likelihood of a victim choosing to report crime.

4. Children and young people fear repercussions of reporting

⇨ Children and young people identify a range of risks associated with reporting crime including reputational damage, implications for their family or fears of significant physical reprisal.

Even where children and young people had a sense that what was happening to them wasn't right and they wanted to report this, evidence from the focus groups indicates a lack of knowledge about the most appropriate way to do this. Several young people voiced uncertainty on how to report incidents where they weren't in immediate danger and didn't feel a 999 call was warranted:

"From what I've seen young people are fairly confident regarding bigger crimes. If it's someone's house gets broken into, that's definitely a thing for the police whereas if it's like bullying and cyber bullying, it's generally approached as the sort of thing that's dealt with by like schools or heads of year and maybe people aren't quite sure how the police would go about that" (female, group 3).

"You need better education about what actually happens when you report a crime...they tell us these numbers – like 999 and 101 – but they don't tell us actually what happens when you call one of those numbers. What do you have to say? What should you expect?" (female, group 2).

⇨ Unwritten group 'rules' in certain social contexts de-legitimise the idea of reporting crime to authorities and in some instances, threats or blackmail by perpetrators exert a significant silencing power over children and young people's likelihood of reporting crime.

5. Children and young people may blame themselves for victimisation

⇨ Many children and young people falsely assume responsibility for their experiences of harm and victimisation. Where children and young people feel in any way responsible for their victimisation they are unlikely to report these experiences or seek support.

⇨ Professionals can also be guilty of reinforcing damaging messages around responsibility to victims through their reactions to disclosure or use of language.

6. Negative perceptions of the police can deter reporting of crime

⇨ Many children and young people have little confidence that the criminal justice system will deliver justice and protect victims.

⇨ Children and young people's attitudes towards the police are often characterised by feelings of mistrust and fear. Many believe that the police treat them more negatively than they do adults and anticipate that their direct contact with the police is likely to be characterised by a lack of respect, suspicion or discrimination.

9 December 2014

⇨ The above information is reprinted with kind permission from Victim Support and the University of Bedfordshire. Please visit www.victimsupport. org.uk for further information.

Young victims of crime: understanding the support you should get

If you're a victim of crime, support and information is available to help you get through it.

The *Victims' Code* is a Government document that tells you what support and information victims of crime in England and Wales should get from criminal justice agencies. These are organisations like the police and the courts. The *Victims' Code* has a special section for people who are under 18 because they should get extra support.

Telling the police about the crime

You can tell the police about a crime by phone, online or by going to the police station. The police should give you information so you know what happens after you've told them about the crime and what support you should get next.

Unless you say you don't want this, the police will give your contact details to a charity that gives help to victims. Someone from the charity will get in touch with you to offer their help or support.

You can have an adult stay with you while the police ask you questions about what happened. This could be your parent or family friend but they need to be over 18 years old.

You may be asked to make something called a witness statement. This is when you say what happened when the crime took place like what time it was and where you were. The police will ask you if you also want to make a Victim Personal Statement (VPS). This is when you say how the crime has made you feel and how it has changed things for you. The VPS lets you tell the judge and others in the court room how you feel about what happened to you.

You don't have to make a VPS if you don't want to, but if you do choose to make one, it can be made at any time before the case goes to court. Once you have made a VPS and signed it, you can't take it back or change it but you can write another one to give more information to the police and courts.

You will be asked if you would like to read your VPS out in court if the suspect is found guilty. You do not have to do this if you don't want to and can ask for somebody else to read it out for you instead. If you don't want your VPS to be read out in court at all, the court will still look at it before they decide what punishment to give to the suspect.

Knowing what's happening

The police should get in touch with you or your parents to let you know how they are looking into the crime and whether anyone has been arrested or charged for the crime.

You can tell the police how often you want to hear from them about the investigation and how you would like to be contacted.

Going to court

If your case does not go to court, you should be told why not. If there is a trial, you may be asked to be a witness in court, this means you will have to speak in court to tell them what happened.

If you are a witness at court, you should be told about what this means for you and should be kept up to date with information with what's happening. This includes:

⇨ information about where and when the court hearings will take place whether the suspect has been allowed to go home until the court date or is being held in prison

Also:

⇨ you may able to visit the court before the day of the trial if you want

⇨ someone from the Witness Care Unit should contact you before you go to court to answer all your questions about going to court and to help you until the case is finished.

After the trial

If you've been a victim of a sexual or violent crime, and the suspect is sent to prison for more than 12 months, you will be able to join the Victim Contact Scheme. Victims on this scheme can get updates on what happens to the suspect after they go to prison and can give their thoughts on any rules the suspect must follow when they come out of prison. If you are under 18, your parent or guardian can decide to use this service to get updates and to pass on your views.

Being a witness

If you go to court as a young witness in a trial you may be able to use 'special measures' to help make it easier for you to tell the court about the crime. Special measures are things like:

⇨ having a screen around the witness box so that you don't have to see the suspect or their family when you are answering questions

⇨ being able to give evidence by live video-link so you don't have to be in the same room as where the trial is taking place

⇨ the judge and lawyers remove their wigs and gowns to make you more comfortable

⇨ having someone, called an intermediary, be with you in court to help you understand the questions you are being asked.

You can also ask people who work at the court if you can wait in an area away from the suspect and their friends and family.

Restorative justice

As a victim you may be able to take part in restorative justice. This is when you have contact with the offender so that both of you can find a way forward and build a more positive future. It gives you a chance to tell them how the crime has affected you so they can understand the impact of their crime. The offender is also able to say why they did the crime and say sorry if they want to. Both you and the offender need to agree to this before it happens. You do not have to take part in Restorative Justice but you will be given lots of support if you decide to write to or meet the offender.

Gary

Gary, 15, attended a restorative justice meeting with the offender who had mugged him:

"At first it felt strange to be so close to the offender. The officer who was there was a big help. Each person had a chance to speak. My family and I talked about how we were affected and so did the guy who mugged me. As he explained what happened and why – basically it was down to drugs, drugs, drugs – our anger went away. We all signed an agreement at the end, which included suggestions and changes that would improve the life of the offender and (hopefully) stop him committing more crimes in future.

"I am glad we attended the conference. The great thing about it was that the offender got to hear what it was like for me and was very sorry. We too got to see into his life and understood better what had driven him to crime."

⇨ The above information is reprinted with kind permission from The Ministry of Justice. Please visit www.gov.uk for further information.

© Crown copyright 2015

Teenage sexting is not all the same – criminalise abuse, not sexual exploration

***An article from* The Conversation.**

By Nikki Godden-Rasul, Lecturer in Law, Newcastle University

THE CONVERSATION

Now that so many teenagers have smartphones equipped with cameras it's inevitable that they're used to take pictures, sometimes regrettable pictures, and to share them with others. The problem is that this is not just often regrettable in their own eyes, but also illegal in the eyes of the law.

A 14-year-old boy who took a naked selfie and sent it to a girl at school that he'd been flirting with recently found himself in hot water with his school and with the police. Both his and the girl's details have been added to a police intelligence database for making and distributing an indecent image. Indecent because, as an image of a minor, it's classified as child pornography under the Protection of Children Act 1978.

The police investigating said no charges were brought as it was not in the public interest. But the boy was informed that this record may,

despite the lack of conviction or charges, be revealed by advanced criminal records checks. This could potentially ruin both of the teenagers' futures if their chosen careers involve working with children.

Criminal 'sexting'?

The case highlights the problems raised by smartphone-enabled 'sexting' that is increasingly common among young people, and yet, where the subject of the image is under 18, constitutes the creation and distribution of child pornography. Children are unnecessarily criminalised, and the broad scope of criminal law discourages schools from educating teenagers about when sharing sexual images may be harmful or a harmless part of teenage sexual exploration. Whether part of growing up or not, teens need to know that all sexting could be seen as potentially criminal.

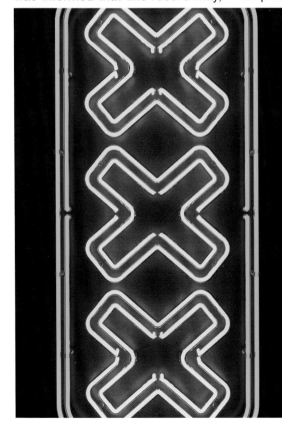

This all-encompassing sweep of the law is recognised as a problem, so CPS guidance limits the prosecution of teenagers sharing images of themselves when they are not causing harm to others. For instance, the approach of the Association of Chief Police Officers is to safeguard children over bringing prosecutions, and in this case the investigating police said no one was arrested or interviewed under caution.

Nevertheless, as the school exercised its discretion to report the incident to the police it was recorded as a crime. While the school says

pupils were informed that this was their policy, the boy in question says he was not aware of this, nor of the consequences of admitting his actions – something he did with police present and without any form of adult representation.

Teenage kicks that have lasting consequences

So now a 14-year-old's name appears in a police crime record, relating to a sexual offence no less, which could damage his future – even though no charge was brought against him. It's likely to be of little comfort that the National Police Chief's Council state that the decision to disclose this under future record checks is "carefully considered" and "in line with Home Office guidance".

This case also raises questions about the scope of offences involving the making and distribution of sexual or intimate images. In particular, how a provision in the Protection of Children Act regarding child pornography, designed to protect children, is being used to criminalise them. The problem is that the law captures incidents that may not be harmful, and distorts the kinds of harm caused in particular circumstances. Teenage sexting is not a problem because it involves naked images of minors. It is a problem when the sharing of sexual images is used in an abusive way.

In this case, for example, if the boy sent the image with the intention of causing distress, as an act of harassment, then this would constitute harm. Alternatively, the boy in this case could be seen as the victim, as the girl who received the image shared it with others, either with the intention to humiliate or without thought to the possibility, and in any case without the boy's consent. This could constitute an offence under the new so-called 'revenge porn' legislation. In fact this more accurately depicts the situation – of more immediate concern to the boy than his record is the humiliation he feels at school that numerous schoolmates have seen the image, and repeatedly refer to it. However, no such offence was recorded.

Criminalising young people for making or distributing such images without taking into account the context only serves to draw attention away from really harmful behaviour – either among teenagers, or from those who might prey upon them.

Young people need to be informed of the law, its implications for sexting, and understand what constitutes ethical and unethical behaviour involving the sharing of sexual images. The sharing of sexual images as harassment or abuse or as acts of 'revenge porn' should be reported. Schools' focus should be to teach teenagers about healthy and harmful sexual relationships. It's particularly apparent that this often occurs in the context of abusive relationships which commonly involve a male perpetrator and female victim. The sexualisation of women and girls too, means images of them are treated differently to that of men and boys.

However, despite the importance of discussing these important issues with teenagers, institutional fear and cultural concerns around offences of a sexual nature and the wide scope of the law that criminalises all sexting as if it were the same too often means the education needed just doesn't happen.

4 September 2015

⇨ The above information is reprinted with kind permission from *The Conversation*. Please visit www.theconversation.com for further information.

New technologies, new victims: Internet offending

The internet offending landscape remains unclear with limited research in this area. This article aims to outline some of the current challenges in this area. New technologies refer to websites, social media, apps and devices, such as smartphones. Some young people's actions online result in them becoming involved in offending behaviour, or finding themselves vulnerable to the behaviours of others.

NSPCC/ChildLine's experience

NSPCC/ChildLine have reported a 65% increase in contact from young people, adults and professionals regarding new technologies. Contacts recorded include a 168% increase in reports of online sexual abuse. Of those young people who have contacted NSPCC their experiences include:

⇨ 12% cyber-stalking

⇨ 12% unwanted sexual messages

⇨ 8% asked to send or respond to a sexual message.

Non-contact offending behaviour

The Sexual Offences (Scotland) Act 2009 defines this as the making, taking or distributing of indecent images of children using digital technologies (in law, having illegal material on a computer or device or obtaining illegal material onto a computer or device, not producing it yourself).

Involvement in non-contact offences can be due to vulnerability through learning needs including autistic spectrum disorder, exploration of sexual identity and orientation or as part of a grooming process. Online pornography addictions are increasingly common in young men; accessing adult pornography online and their behaviour then becoming unregulated.

Contact and non-contact offending behaviour

Some people may view images before going on to commit contact offences, whereas others may not commit contact offences at all. Others may be in possession of illegal images for financial gain only, selling images as a 'business' (CEOP 2012).

A 2011 study measured 30 dual (contact and non-contact) and 30 non-contact adult offenders. Although concluding from a small sample, they suggest differences exist between the two groups, with contact offenders mainly possessing higher leave images on the COPINE scale. The study suggests those with prior convictions for contact offences and also committing non-contact offences were more likely to have access to children and more likely to be opportunistic.

In the most recent meta-analysis, less than 5% of online offenders recidivated during the follow up period, which was up to six months.

Victims

One means of supporting young people to manage pressure and expectations online is ZIPIT, an app developed in association with young people by ChildLine, which prevents some young people becoming victims of online abuse.

May 2015

⇨ The above information is reprinted with kind permission from the Centre for Youth & Criminal Justice. Please visit www.cycj.org.uk for further information.

Social media is driving the rise of hate crime, but it can also stop it

Technology makes it easier for trolls, but also allows society to become more resilient to them.

By Carl Miller

This week candlelit vigils, pop up stands, theatre shows and awareness sessions will appear across the Britain. It is National Hate Crime Awareness Week, a campaign led by Stop Hate UK that sees schools, police forces, civic society groups, national politicians and local governments all come together to raise awareness of crimes directed at people simply because of who they are.

"Social media is changing why hate crime happens..."

Whilst crime in general has been falling for decades, reaching a record low earlier this year, hate crime has gone in the other direction and in London it's increased substantially over the last three years. This is even more worrying given that hate crime is chronically under reported in the official figures. The Crime Survey – a major regular monitor of these kinds of trends – concluded that 43 per cent of hate crimes are not reported to the police. Other research goes higher: Stonewall research for instance found that three quarters of gay, lesbian and bisexual victims of hate crime didn't tell the police.

Hate crime is now a major priority for the police, and forces have published new strategies and mobilised more resources to better reach those that are affected, make it easier to report and (like this campaign) raise the public's awareness and alertness to it.

Hate crime is difficult to tackle for lots of reasons. Some of the groups that are most targeted are also those who have the least confidence in the police and public authorities. Hate crimes also often happen within longer campaigns of harassment – the police call this "repeat victimisation" – and in some cases victims may not report the crime because they fear reprisals from people they suspect they'll see again. However, sitting at the heart of this challenge is a major problem. Hate crime itself has radically changed over the last few years. Along with banking and advertising, hate crime has also gone digital and social media is now the latest frontline in the fight against it.

Most obvious of course has been how social media has changed where hate crime happens. It is a new way to reach a victim in their own home, and campaigns of prejudice and harassment often now have online as well as offline dimensions to them. One of the nastiest breeds of troll focus on the identity of the victim – their race, gender, sexuality and so on – in order to make the abuse as hurtful, as personalised as possible. Labour MP Stella Creasy and Classicist Mary Beard to columnists Hadley Freeman and Grace Dent, many women in public life have pointed out the online abuse they receive is not directed at what they have said or done, but at their gender. Sprinkled in amongst the general abuse and bomb threats has been a recurring motif: misogynistic and sexualised language and – almost invariably – threats of rape.

Whilst the online abuse of those in the public eye is now something of a predictable social rhythm, it doesn't stop at celebrities. At Demos, we've been struggling to get to grips with how much abuse of this kind is happening to normal people. On Twitter (which

is by no means the only venue) we've seen a very sharp increase indeed. We counted how many Tweets contained one of a number of popular racial slurs. In 2012, it was around 10,000 a day. A month ago, it had increased to 480,000. Now, many of these slurs are used by the very people they were originally intended to derogate, and the vast majority certainly will not be hate crime, but nonetheless a 4,800 per cent increase is astonishing – far greater than the general increase in Tweets over that time.

"Whilst crime in general has been falling for decades [...] hate crime has gone in the other direction and in London it's increased substantially over the last three years"

Social media is also changing why hate crime happens. The earliest adopters of new ways of communicating are usually those that are most denied the traditional means, and in the early years of Facebook this was groups like the English Defence League and their far-right cousins across Europe. Facebook handed everyone the ability to set up a group, recruit new members and get the message out to possible follow-travellers, all for free. This has radically widened the kinds of groups that are out there in the UK, including those whose activities and outlooks are regarded by many to be profoundly hateful. These Facebook groups often have had street-based wings, and people are being mobilised more quickly and unpredictably than ever before. The EDL were on the streets hours after the killing of Lee Rigby in 2013. Before social media, they could never have organised so quickly.

The rise of digital crime in general, I suspect, has been a painful, even agonising experience for the police and online hate crime is one important part of this wider enforcement crisis. The Metropolitan Police received around 2,000 complaints last year about online harassment, and predict the problem will get worse. They are not alone, and as forces across the country face soaring numbers of complaints there are big problems with how to keep a society safe that lives increasingly in online worlds.

New expertise is needed to inspect digital crime scenes and track down online perpetrators, but these same skills are in demand elsewhere too – and it's difficult for the police to beat the salaries on offer at major tech companies. Territorial jurisdictions matter a lot less online, and hateful abuse can be thrown at people living in the UK from anywhere in the world, from data havens sat in international waters or – thanks to encryption – from the shadowed areas on the Internet that are beyond the reach of any law altogether.

"[Social media is] a new way to reach a victim in their own home, and campaigns of prejudice and harassment often now have online as well as offline dimensions to them"

No doubt technology will be as central to the solution as it is to the problem of hate crime. Hate Crime Awareness Week uses social media to promote the very values and greater recognition of hate crime that will make our society more resilient to it – there are online toolkits and an interactive map. But to borrow one of that campaign's hashtags, there is much to do before the Internet really is #No Place For Hate.

12 October 2015

⇨ The above information is reprinted with kind permission from *The Telegraph*. Please visit www. telegraph.co.uk for further information.

Lessons from Beyond Youth Custody

"People don't appreciate how much it can feel like you are being set up to fail"

In January 2015, the number of children in custody was 981. The first time on record the population has fallen below 1,000. Numbers have been falling steadily over the past decade, which is welcome, but it poses new and significant challenges for services.

Those sentenced to custody are more likely to display an entrenched pattern of offending behaviour. They're more likely to have committed serious offences and have a higher concentration of problems.

Reoffending rates remain stubbornly high. Over two thirds of children reoffend within 12 months of release from secure institutions. Reoffending rates are also substantially higher amongst young adults in the criminal justice system than older adult offenders. This shows the destructive cycle of crime that some young people fall into and struggle to get out of.

Many of these young people have had complicated and chaotic lives. Many have experienced trauma, abuse, bereavement, grown up in local authority care, been excluded from school, experienced drug- or alcohol-related dependencies and have mental health problems or personality disorders.

Young people are increasingly isolated from family. The closure of some institutions and restructuring of the secure estate has meant some young offenders end up in custody a long way from home.

Gang-involvement is problematic. A recent inspection report by Her Majesty's Inspectorate of Prisons reported that Feltham young offenders' institution was "rife with gang violence" and called for new thinking about how to tackle the "debilitating and seemingly intractable" problem.

Support isn't consistent between youth and adult systems. The transition from the youth justice system to the adult justice system further impacts on the consistency and quality.

Where appropriate support is available and agencies work together in a coordinated way, custody can provide young people with the interventions they need to overcome problems and start the process of building a better life. Central to this is making sure resettlement is the driving force of sentence planning.

All too often it isn't. Services are patchy or poorly coordinated, too little attention is given to preparing young people for release and planning for resettlement doesn't start early enough in their sentence – when it is most effective.

Beyond Youth Custody aims to change this picture. It has been designed to challenge, advance and promote better thinking in policy and practice for the effective resettlement of young people, with the ultimate aim of improving outcomes for young people leaving custody.

Read the report *Effective resettlement of young people: lessons from Beyond Youth Custody* for more information.

⇨ The above information (and the *Youth justice timeline* opposite) is reprinted with kind permission from the Beyond Youth Custody programme. Please visit www.beyondyouthcustody.net for further information.

Tom's story

The first time I ever went to prison I was 15 and still had a long way to go in maturity. I was still caught up in gangs and drugs and I found myself at the beginning of my offending cycle.

At the end of my custodial sentence I was released with no sense of direction and I had to rely on the YOT to support me through my rehabilitation. As part of my licence I was forced to attend pointless meetings and workshops.

When I tried to voice my opinions and reach out for help, I was shunned and my questions were disregarded. They told me, "These are the things we have in place for you. You can choose to attend them or we can breach you and send you back to prison." This made me very disengaged and hostile.

Within a few weeks I was reoffending and soon back in prison. Angry and with no optimism for my release, I found myself constantly getting into fights. On the day of my release I met with someone from the YOT and they gave me my agenda for the week. When I saw what they had planned, I immediately gave up hope.

Youth justice timeline

⇨ **1792** The Royal Philanthropic Society opens a centre in London to take convicted children who might otherwise be transported abroad. In 1797 it starts supporting children after they leave – possibly the first such resettlement scheme.

⇨ **1823** Prison ships are introduced to house some young offenders. Criticised for being harsh and cruel, the last of these hulks closes in 1846.

⇨ **1847** Juvenile Offenders Act is the first legislation to distinguish between adults and children in the justice system. Children under 14 now to be tried summarily in a magistrates court for lesser offences.

⇨ **1854** Youthful Offenders Act allows courts to sentence children under 16 to a stint in a reformatory for between two and five years as an alternative to prison – but they must serve an initial 14 days in prison.

⇨ **1893** Reformatory Schools Act gives courts the option of sending children to reformatories without the initial two weeks in prison. The prison element is finally abolished in the Reformatory Schools Act 1899.

⇨ **1902** The first borstal institution for young males opens on an experimental basis near Rochester in Kent. Sir Evelyn Ruggles-Brise introduces a strict regime based on physical drill, training and education.

⇨ **1908** Children's Act establishes a separate juvenile court for the first time, dealing with both crime and welfare issues, abolishes custody for children below 14, and now requires the police to provide remand homes.

⇨ **1908** Prevention of Crime Act rolls out borstals nationally for males aged 16–20 on an indeterminate sentence between one and three years. Release is followed by a supervised licence period of resettlement in the community.

⇨ **1933** Children and Young Persons Act requires courts to have regard to a child's welfare, raises the age of criminal responsibility to eight years old, and abolishes the death penalty for the under-18s.

⇨ **1952** Detention centres are opened, where sentences of up to three months are intended as a 'short, sharp shock' for 14- to 20-year-olds. The 1948 Act had introduced them to replace court-imposed corporal punishment.

⇨ **1963** Children and Young Persons Act raises the age of criminal responsibility to ten. Responding to the Ingleby report, it also requires local authorities to undertake preventative work with children and families at risk of offending.

⇨ **1969** Children and Young Persons Act introduces supervision orders and care orders. Secure units and approved schools are combined into local authority community homes. Its raising the age of criminal responsibility to 14 is never implemented.

⇨ **1982** Criminal Justice Act merges youth imprisonment and borstals into youth custody centres for the under-21s, restricting use to a last resort. Detention centres are reaffirmed as a short, sharp shock. 'Specified activities' are introduced.

⇨ **1989** UN Convention on the Rights of the Child is published. Article 3 states that children's best interests should always be a primary consideration, and Article 37 limits custody to the shortest possible time.

⇨ **1991** Criminal Justice Act replaces juvenile courts with youth courts and includes 17-year-olds for the first time. The age that the youth court can impose custody is raised from 14 to 15, and curfew orders are introduced for the over-16s.

⇨ **1993** Two-year-old James Bulger is murdered by two 10-year-old boys in Liverpool. The media and public backlash against young people hardens political attitudes to young offenders and influences justice policy for decades.

⇨ **1993** Criminal Justice Act signals a punitive turn for the justice system. It allows more scope for courts to impose tougher sentences, taking into account offender history and offences committed while on bail.

⇨ **1998** Crime and Disorder Act introduces the principal aim for youth justice as being the prevention of offending. It establishes multi-agency youth offending teams and a range of orders. Doli incapax for children under 14 is abolished.

⇨ **1999** Anti-social behaviour orders are introduced following the 1998 Act. These civil court orders are disproportionately received by children, imposing restrictions for sub-criminal behaviour. Breaching is a criminal offence punishable by custody.

⇨ **2000** First set of national standards specific to youth justice is introduced by the Youth Justice Board, defining the minimum required level of service provision from agencies. Funding is conditional on related key performance targets.

⇨ **2008** Criminal Justice and Immigration Act replaces all existing community orders with the youth rehabilitation order, addressing reoffending risk through an individualised intervention package. Requirements for courts to balance the prevention of offending with welfare remain unimplemented.

⇨ **2014** Anti-Social Behaviour Crime and Policing Act replaces anti-social behaviour orders with injunctions for the prevention of nuisance and annoyance (civil) and criminal behaviour orders. In addition to restrictions, the new orders allow courts to impose activity requirements.

Peer court leads the way for youth justice

Reporter Elise Brewerton sits in on an innovative type of court hearing for first-time young offenders aged ten to 17 which is getting great results in preventing re-offending – and is helping victims too.

Of those, many will have received cautions which could stay on their records for up to three years.

But thanks to an innovative scheme, many are avoiding a criminal record and being steered away from further crime and anti-social behaviour through a peer court made up of other young people.

This Saturday marks a year of the Hampshire Community Court, which has been running as a pilot in Fareham and Gosport.

More than 70 cases have been heard by a panel of young people aged 14 to 25, who decide outcomes suitable for young, first-time offenders who have committed low-level crimes.

In the first year just five per cent of the respondents – the perpetrators – have gone on to re-offend. The national figure is 33 per cent.

Last night, at Fareham police station, a panel of young people aged between 15 and 21 heard two cases – an assault by an 11-year-old boy and a theft by a 15-year-old boy.

In order for cases to go before the peer court, both sides have to agree that they want to take part in a restorative process.

It is formal in the sense of where it is held, the panel wear uniforms and both the victim and the respondent have advocates – also young people – speaking on their behalf.

But, unlike a magistrates' court, both sides can discuss the case and ask questions.

The victim in the assault case was a 14-year-old boy who was punched twice by the younger boy.

The peer panel ask careful, considered questions designed to make both the victim and the respondent think hard about the situation and how to resolve it.

The older boy wants to know why he was singled out, why he was abused.

Both parents are able to explain how the crime has affected them too.

The panel deliberate for 15 minutes over how justice can be served and they settle on a written apology.

Afterwards both the victim and his mother are happy with the outcome.

Liam Mills, 19, led the panel. He says: "It's exciting to know we're able to make a difference to our peers' lives".

The results so far have proved the Police and Crime Commissioner Simon Hayes was right to set aside £150,000 of taxpayers' money for the project.

He says: "What it's doing is showing young people the error of their ways, encouraging young people not to reoffend.

"And also it's giving an understanding for the victim as to why the crime was committed.

"What we're finding is both the victim and the perpetrator are very happy with this scheme".

Comment: PC Mark Walsh

The idea for the community court came from PC Mark Walsh. He was inspired by the American system, which has been running for more than 20 years in almost every state.

PC Walsh won a fellowship from the Winston Churchill Memorial Trust to spend six weeks in the USA researching how peer courts work.

When Police and Crime Commissioner Simon Hayes was elected in 2013, PC Walsh went to him for funding and was successful.

It's something Hampshire Constabulary would not have had the budget for, but it has more than likely saved it a lot of money dealing with young people who are diverted away from a life of crime by coming face-to-face with victims.

PC Walsh says: "From an operational perspective I'm very proud of what the volunteers have achieved.

"It's a success for them in terms of the commitment they've given to their community.

"We've only got a five per cent re-offending rate.

"The national re-offending rate is 33 per cent. In those terms it can be deemed a success as well."

He adds: "It's a restorative approach. It doesn't replace anything that the criminal justice system currently does.

"It actually enhances the police outcomes."

Comment: Daisy Brown

Daisy Brown has acted as an advocate for both perpetrators and victims in more than 40 of the 70 cases held so far.

The 18-year-old, from Fareham, is about to head off to university and eventually wants to be a solicitor.

She says: "Most of the kids we get in here are not bad kids, they have just made a mistake.

"That's why the programme is so effective.

"We don't want them to be branded as trouble-makers because of one error of judgment.

"All the victims we have met have been satisfied.

"It's a lot more personal than a real courtroom. They can ask questions. You don't get that opportunity in a proper court.

"It's good that they get to put their point of view across.'

All the young people involved in the community court are volunteers.

Daisy adds: " I really enjoy it. It's good for my confidence. A year ago I couldn't stand up in a room full of people and do this.

"It's a great experience because you meet lots of different people."

9 September 2015

⇨ The above information is reprinted with kind permission from Portsmouth News. Please visit www.portsmouth.co.uk for further information.

Criminalising ten-year-olds is no way to run a justice system

THE CONVERSATION

An article from **The Conversation.**

By Nicola Carr, Lecturer in Criminology, Queen's University Belfast

At age ten, children in England, Northern Ireland and Wales can be found guilty of a criminal offence. They can face trial and be placed in detention.

We don't allow children of ten to hold a driver's licence or get married or travel on a plane unaccompanied – we don't even allow them to be left at home alone. Yet we treat them as responsible enough for their own actions – and indeed as significantly *au fait* with the law – to face court if they commit a crime.

Children of this age cannot consent to sex – for this you have to be 16. Yet our criminal laws mean that children from age ten upwards can be charged with a sexual offence. There is something very contradictory here.

The age of criminal responsibility in England, Northern Ireland and Wales is well below the average of other countries in the European Union – which is 14. In The Netherlands children cannot be charged with an offence below the age of 12. In France it is 13, in Sweden it is 15. In Belgium the age of criminal responsibility is 18.

Rare cases shouldn't set the age

While the youth justice system operates separately from the adult criminal justice system, its processes largely mirror it. The consequences for a young person when they enter the criminal justice system mirror those of adults too.

In countries with a higher age of criminal responsibility, young people whose behaviour is causing concern are dealt with in the child protection and welfare system. This approach reflects wider social and cultural attitudes towards children and young people. The same goes for England, Wales and Northern Ireland.

Those who resist calls to raise the age invariably point towards the case of James Bulger, the toddler murdered by two ten-year-old boys in 1993. The crime provoked a strong public reaction and the boys eventually became the youngest convicted murderers in modern English history. But the UK Government was challenged in the European Court of Human Rights over the way it treated these young defendants.

While evoking understandable concern, incidents as serious as the Bulger murder are extremely rare. And where they do occur they are invariably symptomatic of deeper problems and need. They should not form the basis for setting the age of criminal responsibility.

Out and staying out

International evidence shows that offending by young people is best addressed by keeping them out of the criminal justice system. Once inside it, there are all kinds of negative consequences – not least being labelled a 'young offender'.

What's more, the range of circumstances under which a criminal record can be disclosed is widening and it is possible for criminal records acquired as a juvenile to follow a person for the rest of their life.

This has profound implications for a young person's educational opportunities and employment prospects. We know that many of the young people that are processed through the youth justice system already suffer the consequences of this.

Groups are emerging to call for the age of criminal responsibility to be raised and I would argue that 16 is more in line with other responsibilities.

Suggesting that the age of criminal responsibility should be raised does not mean ignoring behaviours of concern. It means precisely the opposite. Rather than labelling and punishing children and young people, support should be provided to help them and their families.

20 February 2015

⇨ The above information is reprinted with kind permission from *The Conversation*. Please visit www.theconversation.com for further information.

Prison: the facts

Bromley Briefings Summer 2014.

Facts and figures provide a better basis than tough political rhetoric or media scaremongering for policy and practice change. The facts chart the extraordinary rise in prison numbers over the last 20 years, inflation in sentencing and the social and economic consequences of overuse of custody. Revealing as they do the state of our overcrowded prisons and the state of people in them, the impact of drastic budget cuts and the pace and scale of change in the justice system these figures, drawn largely from government sources, indicate the scope for community solutions to crime.

Opinion polls show strong public backing for measures that reduce crime and disorder from better supervision of young people by their parents to making amends to victims, from mental health and social care to treatment for addictions. It's time to put prison back where it belongs – as an important place of absolute last resort in the justice system.

On 23 May 2014, the prison population in England and Wales was 84,305.[1]

Between June 1993 and June 2012 the prison population in England and Wales increased by 41,800 prisoners to over 86,000.[2]

The prison system as a whole has been overcrowded in every year since 1994.

At the end of March 2014, 77 of the 119 prisons in England and Wales were overcrowded.[3]

Prison has a poor record for reducing reoffending – 46% of adults are reconvicted within one year of release.

For those serving sentences of less than 12 months this increases to 58%. Over two-thirds (67%) of under-18-year-olds are reconvicted within a year of release.[4] Reoffending by all recent ex-prisoners in 2007–08 cost the economy between £9.5 and £13 billion.[5]

37,527 people entered prison in 2013 to serve sentences of less than, or equal to, six months.[6]

Court Orders (Community Orders and Suspended Sentence Orders) are more effective (by nearly 7%) at reducing one-year proven reoffending rates than custodial sentences of less than 12 months for similar offenders.[7]

The average annual overall cost of a prison place in England and Wales for 2012–13 was £36,808.[8]

This has fallen since 2008–09 from £45,000.[9]

40% of prisoners are now held in prisons of 1,000 places or more.[10]

The ratio of prison officers to prisoners in 2000 was 1:2.9, by the end of September 2013 this had increased to 4.8 prisoners for each prison officer.[11]

According to the National Audit Office, there is no consistent correlation between prison numbers and levels of crime.[12]

Approximately 200,000 children in England and Wales had a parent in prison at some point in 2009.[13]

This is more than double the number of children affected in the same year by divorce in the family.[14]

Fewer than 1% of all children in England are in care,[15] but looked after children make up 33% of boys and 61% of girls in custody.[16]

In 2013 there were 215 deaths in custody, the highest number on record.[17]

⇨ The above information is reprinted with kind permission from the Prison Reform Trust. Please visit www.prisonreformtrust.org.uk for further information.

© Prison Reform Trust 2015

7 Table A1, Ministry of Justice (2013) 2013 Compendium of reoffending statistics and analysis, London: Ministry of Justice

8 Table 1, Ministry of Justice (2013) Costs per place and costs per prisoner by individual prison, National Offender Management Service Annual Report and Accounts 2012–13: Management Information Addendum, London: Ministry of Justice

9 Table 2a, Ibid. and Hansard HC, 3 March 2010, c1251W

10 Prison Reform Trust (2013) 'Nearly half of all prisoners to be warehoused in 1,000 plus super sized jails' available at http://www.prisonreformtrust.org.uk/PressPolicy/News/vw/1/ItemID/198

11 Hansard HC, 23 July 2007, c785W and Deposited paper–DEP2014-0327

12 National Audit Office (2012) Comparing International Criminal Justice Systems, London: National Audit Office

13 Ministry of Justice (2012) Prisoners' childhood and family backgrounds, London: Ministry of Justice

14 Office for National Statistics (2011) Divorces in England and Wales 2009, Fareham: Office for National Statistics

15 Department for Education (2013) Children looked after in England year ending 31 March 2013, London: DfE, StatsWales website, and Office for National Statistics (2013) Population Estimates Total Persons for England and Wales and Regions–Mid-1971 to Mid-2012, London: ONS

16 Kennedy, E. (2013) Children and Young People in Custody 2012–13, London: HM Inspectorate of Prisons and Youth Justice Board

17 Table 1.1, Ministry of Justice (2014) Safety in Custody Statistics Quarterly Update to December 2013, London: Ministry of Justice

1 Ministry of Justice (2014) Population and Capacity Briefing for Friday 23 May 2014, London: Ministry of Justice

2 Ministry of Justice (2013) Story of the prison population: 1993–2012 England and Wales, London: Ministry of Justice

3 Ministry of Justice (2014) Monthly Population Bulletin March 2014, London: Ministry of Justice

4 Tables 18a, 18b, 19a, Ministry of Justice (2014) Proven re-offending statistics quarterly July 2011 to June 2012, London: Ministry of Justice

5 National Audit Office (2010) Managing offenders on short custodial sentences, London: The Stationery Office

6 Table A2.1a, Ministry of Justice (2014) Offender Management Statistics Annual Tables 2013, London: Ministry of Justice

UK's first 'supersized' Titan jail to be run by public prison service

Facility under construction in Wrexham will not be run by private sector but will outsource around a third of its services.

By Alan Travis, home affairs editor

Britain's first 'supersized' Titan prison, which will hold more than 2,100 inmates, is to be run by the public prison service and not a private security company.

The prisons minister, Andrew Selous, told MPs on Tuesday that the new £212 million facility being built in Wrexham, North Wales, will be operated by the prison service "as part of an innovative new approach".

The approach does, however, include the outsourcing of a third of the prison's services.

The announcement follows a plea from the Chief Inspector of Prisons for lessons to be learned from the teething troubles at the last major jail to open, Oakwood prison near Wolverhampton, which holds 1,600 inmates and is run by G4S. An early inspection report described it as a prison where it was easier to get hold of illegal drugs than a bar of soap.

Selous said in a written ministerial statement: "Our combination of benchmarking and outsourcing services is saving taxpayers around £300 million a year and now it will allow us to deliver a truly efficient prison in Wrexham that is based on best practice from the opening of previous prisons."

Construction of the new facility on the site of a former Firestone factory started in December. The first housing block is expected to open in two years' time and the jail to be fully operational by September 2017.

Selous said the overall ownership and management of the prison would be in the public sector, but 34% of the services provided would be outsourced to private companies and voluntary organisations. This will include a large industrial complex of 12 workshops.

The Wrexham jail is the first Titan prison to be built in Britain. The last Labour Government was forced to scrap plans to build three Titan jails capable of housing 2,500 inmates each in 2009 after a sustained campaign by penal reformers.

Since then a new generation of 'supersized jails' that can accommodate 1,000-plus inmates has been developed, in some cases by building housing blocks within existing prison perimeters. The average capacity of new prisons built in England and Wales in the last century was about 600.

The shadow justice secretary, Sadiq Khan, said: "Given the mess David Cameron's government made when they handed over the running of brand new Oakwood prison to G4S it's no surprise they don't want to repeat the same mistake. This was a jail where the chief inspector said was easier to get drugs than soap. We don't want that disgraceful failure repeated elsewhere."

Penal reformers observed that the decision to run the Wrexham jail, which has yet to be named, as a public sector prison may have been taken partly to appease the Welsh Assembly. At least one Assembly member, Aled Roberts, the Liberal Democrat member for North Wales, welcomed the decision on Monday.

⇨ The above information is reprinted with kind permission from *The Guardian*. Please visit www.theguardian.com for further information.

Could children in prisons be the next abuse scandal?

If the last few years taught us anything, it's that child abuse thrives in institutions where they can't speak out, are unwilling to do so, or won't be believed when they do.

To a certain extent, it is inevitable. Children are resistant to talking about what is happening right now. Very often, they distrust all adults, and don't differentiate between a social worker and a prison officer. In scandal after scandal, they report abuse years after it has taken place.

But that means authorities must be more imaginative about how to respond. We can encourage children to speak out, and minimise the likelihood of abuse in the first place, by investigating the reality of sex behind bars and following the evidence. That is not happening.

Independent investigators are barred from entering prisons. The Ministry of Justice has made it all but impossible for journalists or researchers to get into jails. *The Guardian* recently spent eight months seeking permission for one reporter to go into an institution. It was denied. The Howard League-organised commission into sex and rape behind bars requested authorisation to conduct a survey on the subject among prisoners. They were denied. We don't have the culture of openness necessary to study the prevalence of abuse in prison.

It's particularly important to get people into prisons or institutions holding young people, because we know the children are unlikely to report abuse to the staff themselves. A survey by the inspector of prisons and the Youth Justice Board found only a third would tell staff if they were being victimised by other children or by staff.

In its interviews with former prisoners, the commission received evidence of alleged abuse by prison staff in the 1960s and 1990s, none of which had been reported at the time. As in Medomsley detention centre, where hundreds of men have now reported to the police that they were abused, it is unlikely the reports emerge until it is too late.

There are people for children to speak to in the current system. Some have access to independent advocates. There is a formal complaints system and social workers in the prison for them to make an independent referral. They also have access to the Samaritans. Perhaps this is all we can do, but allowing in independent investigators would at the very least prove reassuring.

In the US, there is a newfound political focus on sex in prison. Their Review Panel on Prison Rape found 9.5% of children in custody reported one or more incidents of sexual victimisation in prison during the past year. Of these, 2.5% reported being victimised by another child and 7.7% by a member of staff.

The size of the institution is important. The smaller it is, the less likely there is to be abuse. The US panel found facilities holding over 100 inmates were nearly five times as likely to report victimisation as facilities holding fewer than ten. That's very disturbing in a UK context. All prisons for boys in England hold more than 130 children. The 'secure college' the Government is pressing ahead with will hold over 300.

This is a baffling decision to have made. It goes against all the expert advice. Abuse is less likely to take place, and more likely to be reported, in small centres where staff can take a mentoring or teaching role over the children.

But going against the evidence is now par for the course. There is little information coming from the prison estate and little research done by authorities. Neither the National Offender Management Service nor the Youth Justice Board were able to supply information on the number of official complaints of sexual abuse in custody or the number of investigations, criminal charges or convictions following a complaint.

Instead it was forced to send a letter to *Inside Times*, the prison magazine, asking for people to write in describing their experiences. It then relied on evidence from voluntary and statutory agencies, prison governors, former prisoners, HM Inspector of Prisons, the Prisons and Probation Ombudsman, child psychologists and academics to put together today's report.

At the heart of the report is a simple idea: maturing in prison can be a brutalising experience. At the exact point where young people should be going through character-forming sexual and romantic experiences, they are trapped in a hyper-masculine environment, where sexual contact and physically intimacy are impossible.

A majority of these children have experienced multiple disadvantages, such as emotional or mental health issues or deprivation. Over a third have experienced abuse, neglect or been put on the child protection register. 28 per cent have witnessed domestic violence.

Prisons are violent places. Official research found a third of boys in prison felt unsafe at some point and a fifth said they'd been victimised, usually by being hit, kicked or assaulted. At Feltham prison, for instance, there was an average of two fights or assaults every day, including pre-meditated group attacks on individual boys.

Children are often disciplined for perfectly normal sexual behaviour, like masturbation or the possession of magazines like *Nuts* or *Zoo*. Homophobia was, predictably, very common.

We just don't know very much about the effect of prison on young people, but the evidence we do have suggests it brutalises them, trapping them in an aggressive environment without role models at a crucial period of their development. The evidence suggests it may very well increase the chances of them becoming sexual offenders later in life. There is a very strong argument to suggest that we should never imprison young people and that if we must it should be in very small institutions – certainly not the child super-prison the Coalition is inexplicably pushing forward.

There is no reason to question the good intentions and professionalism of the staff who work with young people in prisons. But unless we have a culture of openness around detention – and are prepared to follow the evidence it throws up – we will not have done everything in our power to prevent abuse.

A Ministry of Justice spokesperson said:

"Prison inspectors and criminal justice experts visit prisons on a regular basis in order to scrutinise and conduct legitimate and important research. We take all assaults in prisons extremely seriously, monitoring all incidents and publishing data on a regular basis.

"We work closely with the police to help facilitate criminal investigations and all establishments for young offenders are subject to independent scrutiny, with safeguarding issues among the specific areas assessed."

10 February 2015

⇨ The above information is reprinted with kind permission from Politics.co.uk.

Babies behind bars

By Maya Oppenheim

Pregnancy can be an anxious experience for all women: fears of miscarrying, birth defects, difficult labour and how you'll cope are natural when you're carrying a child. If you're pregnant in prison, however, natural anxieties can become terrifying. What happens if you can't get proper healthcare? What happens if you're not let out of your cell when your waters break? What happens if you miscarry and no one knows what to do?

Being pregnant in prison comes with myriad fears – most distressing of all is the question of whether you will be able to keep your baby. While female prisoners are legally allowed to keep their baby for the first 18 months in a secure Mother and Baby Unit, the vast majority of children are separated from their mothers. In turn, many women go into labour knowing that their baby will be lifted from their arms within hours, that they will return to prison later alone, swollen and lactating.

According to the NSPCC's latest report, an average of 100 babies are born in prisons in England and Wales each year. Yet antenatal care in prisons remains substandard. Not only is there no universal standard for what prisons have to provide for pregnant women, there is no legal requirement to offer antenatal classes. You might be bearing a child but you're a prisoner at all times. Evidence has shown, too, that women inside are more likely to experience birth defects or have stillborn babies than those on the outside.

Maddie Logan*, 30, from Bristol, has experienced the ills of our prison system first-hand. For the entirety of her pregnancy, she was told she would not be able to keep her child. "I suffered from depression for the whole nine months because I was told I wouldn't be allowed to keep my baby," she tells me.

Two weeks overdue, Maddie's labour was defined by fear. "For 14 days I'd been sitting in the prison, overdue, before they finally transported me to hospital in a van to induce me," she says. "In labour, nothing was working. First they gave me tablets, but that didn't work. Then they broke my waters, but that didn't work either. Eventually then they put me on a higher-dose drip."

It was only when the prison officer came in and told Maddie that she could keep her baby that "it came out straight away". Within 30 minutes, Ruby Logan* came into the world, within touching distance of two prison guards.

"It was horrible having two people I barely knew with me at all times. Especially in such a tiny room that only had enough space for a small hospital bed with two chairs at the end," Maddie recalls. "Imagine waking up to deal with a crying baby in the night and, right at the end of your bed, you see two men officers watching you. You would have thought they'd at least stand outside the door. It's not like you can escape. The small windows didn't even open."

Maddie's entire pregnancy was plagued by uncertainty. "I thought I'd have to hand her out to a family member and not see her for over two and a half years, until I'd finished my sentence," she explains. "I was scared about all sorts of other things, too. When I'd press my buzzer and nobody would come, I'd get paranoid that the same thing would happen when I needed to go into labour.

"I was also frightened that I'd miscarry or that they wouldn't call my family in time for the birth. Ah god," she exhales, deeply. "All the worries got me down. It's not like being pregnant on the outside. It's a lot more pressure. If you get scared, you can't just go see a doctor, you have to wait."

Maddie is adamant that she received no special treatment as a mother-to-be in prison. "They weren't nicer to me because I was pregnant. I'd have my regular scans inside the prison, but they don't keep an extra eye on you. I had no antenatal classes. There were no special mattresses. If I cried and got upset, all they'd do was get an officer to come and sit with me and

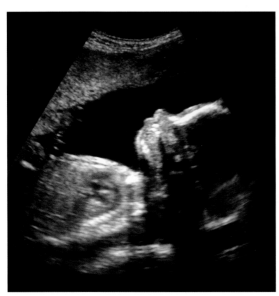

that was it. I won't put them all down, but most don't really care. They're just there to do their job."

Arrested for attempting to smuggle drugs and a phone into prison for a friend, Maddie was initially told she'd get five years. But this was dropped to three and a half years when the judge found out she was pregnant. "I was two weeks pregnant when I got caught smuggling. They nicked me straight away and I was put on remand and sentenced after a few weeks," she explains. A former heroin addict, Maddie was smuggling drugs in to pay off debts. "It's a long story, but I was bullied into taking it in for someone because I owed a lot of money, and then the debt would've been wiped off."

During her sentence, Maddie was moved from Holloway in London to Bronzefield and then back to Eastwood Park where there was a Mother and Baby Unit. "It was a lot better than prison," she says. "You could go outside and walk around the grounds with your baby. It's obviously fenced off but there's a big garden. You've got to be in your room at certain times but you have keys to your own door. It's not like you get locked in with your baby."

Without Ruby, Maddie says she wouldn't have been able to cope. Having her with her kept her going. "I just wish they hadn't waited till the last moment to tell me that I'd be allowed to keep her. I understand they've got to do checks – if I'd been in prison for violence before, I wouldn't have been able to go to the unit – but I hadn't".

Maddie and Ruby were finally released from the Mother and Baby Unit in 2010 when Ruby was six and a half months old. "Ruby is five now and is doing really well," says Maddie. "She's absolutely lovely. She doesn't remember anything from the prison, but I suppose I'll have to tell her when she's older."

Maddie is not alone in her experience. The latest figures show that two babies are born in prison every week. Despite this, the physical and psychological needs of pregnant women continue to be neglected. From the chief inspector and head governor to the wing officers, prison is an institution designed by men, for men.

Moreover, lots of women only find out they are pregnant after their preliminary health check-up. In turn, they are forced to deal with this news on their first night behind bars. Mothers-to-be are housed in standard prison accommodation, sleeping on wafer-thin plastic mattresses with threadbare blankets. Forced to eat whatever custodial cuisine is thrown at them – in spite of inexplicable cravings – like everyone else they must navigate the punitive, rigid routine of prison. If they have morning sickness and skip breakfast, a mid-morning round of dry toast isn't really an option.

As well as inadequate food and nutrition, evidence has shown that persistent institutional failures lead to substandard antenatal care and a lack of emotional support. In a recent study of 1,082 mothers in prison estates in England, almost two thirds reported that they were depressed and that 56 per cent were lonely.

Miscarriage is another devastating issue, albeit one that has little coverage. Public Health England does not record statistics on miscarriages across the prison estate. In spite of this, miscarriage is thought to be widespread, with chilling stories of women being forced to clean up their own blood. Miscarrying is traumatic, painful and a heartbreaking experience in the comfort of your

home or a hospital room. But in a cold concrete cell, alone, it is a living nightmare.

Clive Chatterton, one of the country's most experienced prison governors, has also experienced the failings of the prison system first-hand – from the other side of the bars. Chatterton, 62, started working as a screw at the infamous Strangeways Prison in the 70s, before going on to work at 13 different prisons and serving as the chief governor at three of them. He retired in 2012.

In the 37 years he worked in our prison system, Chatterton says he has was most haunted by his time as governor of Styal, a woman's prison. In his letter to former justice secretary, Ken Clarke, he writes: "I have never come across such a concentration of damaged, fragile and complex-needs individuals".

"Styal was a real eye-opener," he tells me. "We housed 460 women and sometimes over 40 women might be pregnant at any one time. They'd all be at different stages of their pregnancy. Pregnant women would often apply for our on-site Mother and Baby Unit but, if they were refused a place, their babies would often go into care. Staff used to say watching this separation after 18 months together was one of the most traumatic experiences they'd ever seen."

Chatterton also tells me that many women chose not to apply for places in Mother and Baby Units. Instead, they would leave the child with relatives. "Distance was another thing which put women off applying. If Styal was full, they'd be applying for a place which could be 100 miles away from their family."

Perhaps fittingly, Styal is an old Victorian orphanage. Unlike other institutions of its kind, its recent inspections have been positive. "The rooms are brightly coloured like you'd have at a kids nursery, but not too much because obviously the mum is in there as well," says Chatterton. "There's a crèche and nannies who would take the babies for walks outside of the prison and daily visits were allowed."

While Chatterton might be positive about the Mother and Baby Unit, he remains insistent that prison is not the right environment for a mother-to-be. "Let's face it, prison is not the greatest place for anyone to be, and one would say that it's less conducive to someone if they're pregnant. Especially when you remember that most women are sent to prison for non-violent, low-level offending."

As the women's prison population continues to grow – increasing by over a third in the last decade – more and more infants are being separated from their mothers. Even though there are eight Mother and Baby Units in the UK, with a joint capacity of 73 mothers and their babies in total, rejection rates are sky high. According to a recent report by the NSPCC, "Places are under-utilised and frequently lie empty across the women's estate." In 2013, there were only 38 mothers resident in MBUs – just over half the capacity.

Why are these units so under-used? Rigid risk assessment and security criteria mean applications are frequently rejected. On top of this, many women choose not to apply in the first place. This might be because they have been told their application will be refused, or, perhaps they believe that prison is the wrong place for a baby. They may also not want to move far away from family or their older children.

Whatever the reason, the prison system continues to disrupt maternal relationships irreparably. Even in situations when the mother is reunited with their baby on release, they will have missed important stages in their child's development. The infant will now be attached to another caregiver and the mother might feel like a stranger.

It goes without saying that, when you imprison a pregnant woman, you're also imprisoning her – entirely innocent – baby. And, behind bars, this baby is denied the safe, stimulating environment it deserves. Unsurprisingly, the long-term affects on their physical, social and emotional development can be significant.

The same can be said for the children who are left behind when a woman is locked up. After all, two thirds of female prisoners have children under 16, while a third have a child under five. In due course, 17,000 children are separated from their mothers each year because of imprisonment, and it's estimated that 3,000 of them are under the age of two. Out of these children, only five per cent are able to remain in their own home.

In spite of this, the children of prisoners continue to be an invisible group, apparently unworthy of our attention. Universal health and early years services will not necessarily know that a baby has a parent in prison, either. But as life goes on, children of prisoners suffer – they are twice as likely to have mental health problems as their peers.

As a highly vulnerable, troubled demographic plagued by domestic violence, mental health problems and addiction, it's clear that female offenders need help – not the rigid torment of punishment, Not only have half of women in prison experienced domestic violence, 53 per cent have been victims of childhood abuse, and over a third have experienced sexual abuse. Moreover, of the 3,959 women who are currently in prison in Britain, over eight in ten are inside for non-violent crimes, and are far less likely than male prisoners to have any previous convictions.

As a result, Alex Hewson from the Prison Reform Trust argues that, "Pregnant women should not be sent to prison in the first place. It's not the right place environment for a child to be growing."

In the words of Dostoevsky, "A society should be judged not by how it treats its outstanding citizens but by how it treats its criminals."

* Maddie and Ruby's names have been changed.

@MayaOppenheim

18 March 2015

⇨ The above information is reprinted with kind permission from Vice. Please visit www.vice.com for further information.

Time to end the scandal of young people dying in prison

By Frances Crook

The review by Lord Harris of Haringey into the self-inflicted deaths of young adults aged 18–24 in custody is a magisterial overview of the failings in the system. It is the most comprehensive analysis of why so many young people are dying in our prisons ever undertaken.

The final report notes that 101 people in this age group have died in prisons between 2007 and 2014. So far, in 2015, the Howard League is aware of another nine young people who have taken their own lives behind bars.

There are challenging findings for the new Government to consider. Lord Harris rightly asks fundamental questions, such as why so many of these young adults were in custody in the first place. Prison should be used as a last resort. It remains a hugely expensive way to guarantee failure and yet cuts to budgets and staffing mean that whatever hope that prisons might be places of rehabilitation is faint indeed. The review describes an environment where young adults spend too much of their time locked in their cells "not sufficiently engaged in purposeful activities", with their time "not spent in a constructive and valuable way".

The Harris review is also damning of political interference in the safe running of prisons. The last Government's ill-advised changes to the Incentives and Earned Privileges scheme, in order to make prisons more punitive, earns particular criticism.

These changes led to restrictions in access to books and the Books For Prisoners campaign, which is indirectly referred to by the review. In particular, it is noted that the court judgment which ruled the restrictions unlawful makes explicit reference to the importance of rehabilitation. Leadership on providing more effective support for vulnerable people in prison must come from the top.

Hot on the heels of Harris, the Howard League has published a report with the Transition to Adulthood Alliance (T2A), You can't put a number on it, which explores maturity for young adults in the criminal justice system. It draws on participation work involving over 80 18–24-year-olds with experience of the criminal justice system from across England and Wales.

An important lesson from the report is that everyone matures at a different rate and that maturity has little to do with age or legal status. Maturity is complicated. As one young man doing group-work in a prison told us: "I think adulthood begins at different ages for different people". There is mounting evidence that young people develop both neurologically and physically well into their twenties and that some of those changes affect their behaviour and their ability to cope with the punitive and often infantilising setting of prison.

The criminal justice system should be better at giving young people responsibility so they can grow and develop, including help with interpersonal and practical life skills.

Young people want solutions based around them as individuals and which adapt with them as they grow.

A particular concern raised by many young people who spoke to the Howard League was that of the so-called 'paper self', the identity constructed for them by the criminal justice system at a time when they are still finding out who they are. Bureaucratic assessments contained within pre-sentence reports, sentencing remarks, police records or assessments in prison can become the basis for all professional interaction with young people. Young people described facing prejudice based on what staff read and not the person they met, or hearing inaccuracies about close family members based on documents that were no longer up to date.

Harris echoes the Howard League's findings around maturity and supports the T2A contention that maturity should be a primary consideration in making decisions relating to all aspects of how young adults are treated by the criminal justice system.

The review makes various recommendations to ensure consistent and appropriate professional support when young people are imprisoned.

The important question now is: what happens next? A challenge has been placed before Michael Gove at the Ministry of Justice, and before judges, magistrates, prisons, the Crown Prosecution Service and police. If the Harris review is to achieve something meaningful for our troubled young people, then everyone has to play their part in building the change that will save lives.

Frances Crook is Chief Executive of the Howard League for Penal Reform.

3 July 2015

⇨ The above information is reprinted with kind permission from Politics.co.uk.

The Offender Rehabilitation Act

The Offender Rehabilitation Act[1] (ORA) is the Act of Parliament which accompanies the Transforming Rehabilitation programme. The Act makes changes to the sentencing and releasing framework to extend probation supervision after release to offenders serving short-term sentences. It also creates greater flexibility in the delivery of sentences served in the community.[2]

Reduction of unconditional release

Previously, adults serving custodial sentences of less than 12 months were released unconditionally after one half of their sentence had been served.

Under the ORA adults serving custodial sentences of less than 12 months, for an offence committed after 1 February 2015, will be released on licence after serving one half of their sentence in prison and will serve the remaining period in the community.

Introduction of a new supervision period

The ORA introduces a new period of post sentence supervision for all offenders sentenced to less than two years in custody.

Offenders sentenced to less than two years and released on licence, as outlined above, will be subject to an additional period of supervision, for the purposes of rehabilitation once their licence period comes to an end. The licence and supervision periods will together make up 12 months.

Depending on the length of the custodial sentence, the length of the supervision period can vary significantly:

1 Parliament UK (2015) Offender Rehabilitation Act 2014, Online: http://services.parliament.uk/bills/2013-14/offenderrehabilitation.html (last accessed 2.04.2015)

2 The Prison Reform Trust published a number of briefings at each stage of The Offender Rehabilitation Act's passage through parliament. You can download these from http://www.prisonreformtrust.org.uk/PressPolicy/Parliament/Legislation

⇨ Offender A is sentenced to two months in custody, he serves one month in prison, one month on licence and receives an additional 11 months post sentence supervision.

⇨ Offender B is sentenced to 18 months in prison. He serves nine months of this sentence in custody and is then released to serve the remaining nine months in the community, on license. In addition, after his 18 month sentence comes to an end he receives a further three months supervision in the community.

The new supervision period also applies to individuals who are released immediately after sentencing due to the time they have already served on remand.

⇨ Offender C has served six months on remand, at trial he is sentenced to six months in prison. He is released immediately, and then receives a further 12 months supervision.

The only exceptions include: those sentenced to one day and who are therefore not taken into custody, for example, fine defaulters; those aged under 18 on the last day of their custodial period; and those who committed their offence before 1 February 2015.

Supervision requirements may include:

⇨ a requirement to be of good behaviour and not to behave in a way which undermines the purpose of the supervision period;

⇨ a requirement not to commit any further offence;

⇨ a requirement to keep in touch with the supervisor in accordance with the instructions of the supervisor;

⇨ a requirement to reside permanently at an address approved by the supervisor and to obtain the prior permission of the supervisor for any stay of one or more nights at a different address;

⇨ a requirement not to undertake work, or a particular type of work, unless it is approved by the supervisor and to notify the supervisor in advance of any proposal to undertake work or a particular type of work;

⇨ a requirement not to travel outside the British Islands, except with prior permission of the supervisor or in order to comply with a legal obligation;

⇨ a requirement to participate in activities in accordance with any instructions given by a supervisor;

⇨ a drug testing requirement (see below);

⇨ a drug appointment requirement (see below).

Drug testing and drug appointments

The ORA allows for problematic drug use to be tackled as part of an offender's period of supervision on release. It extends previous provision to impose drug testing requirements for Class A drugs to also include Class B drugs. In addition, it introduces a new power to require offenders, on release, to attend appointments designed to address their dependency on, or propensity to, misuse a controlled drug.

Young adult offenders

Those under 18 years old at the point of sentencing but who reach 18 before release will also be subject to the new licence and supervision periods.

This means that young adults could receive variable sentences depending on when they reach their 18th birthday:

⇨ Offenders D and E are both under 18 at the time of their offence. They are arrested together and convicted of the same crime, receiving the same sentence. However, offender D is one day older than offender E, meaning that on release offender D is 18 whereas offender E is 17. Offender D will receive one year supervision in the community under the adult justice system whereas offender E will serve their sentence entirely within the youth justice system.[3]

Female offenders

The ORA states that in providing supervision or rehabilitation the Secretary of State must comply with the public sector equality duty under the Equality Act 2010 as it relates to female offenders and must also identify anything in the arrangements that is intended to meet the particular needs of this group.

Offender F is a woman released from prison who after completing a period on licence in the community is subject to an additional supervision period of six months. The Community Rehabilitation Company responsible for her supervision must ensure that it meets her particular needs as a woman.

April 2015

⇨ The above information is reprinted with kind permission from Clinks. Please visit www.clinks.org for further information.

How to reduce the prison population in one easy step   THE CONVERSATION

***An article from* The Conversation.**

By Robert Canton, Professor in Community and Criminal Justice, De Montfort University

Alarm is spreading once again about the state of UK prisons, with reports that more than 15,000 assaults were committed by prisoners in 2013–14. Justice Minister Chris Grayling might be quick to argue that the violence, suicides and staff shortage represent a "challenge" rather than a crisis but it's time to think seriously about how to reduce the numbers of people in prison.

Attempts are consistently being made to address this problem but each falls flatter than the last. If we simply reduced prison sentences though, we could dramatically reduce overcrowding.

It is generally agreed that overcrowded prisons are bad for everybody – they lead to dangerous and squalid conditions for inmates, as well as staff, and prisoners often have to be moved around, away from their families and the communities in which they will live when they are released. In fact, overcrowding makes it almost impossible to do anything worthwhile with prisoners.

Programmes designed to bring about changes to reduce reoffending certainly take place, but despite the best efforts of many skilled and dedicated staff, there are far more people who need such interventions than there are programmes for them to attend. So much for the rehabilitation revolution.

If current trends continue, all UK prisons will be able to do is to detain people. And even that becomes harder as conditions deteriorate and people become increasingly frustrated and angry. As a report produced after the 1990 riots in Strangeways Prison in Manchester concluded, security,

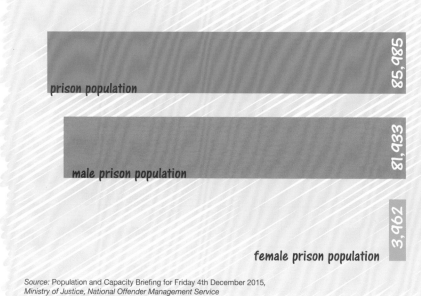

Prison population, December 2015

prison population — 85,985

male prison population — 81,433

female prison population — 3,462

Source: Population and Capacity Briefing for Friday 4th December 2015, Ministry of Justice, National Offender Management Service

discipline and justice are closely linked. If inmates do not feel they are being treated fairly, a prison is likely to experience disorder.

Wrong direction

There are several options that have already been explored for tackling overcrowding. Each generally ends in disappointment.

Increasing capacity is a bad idea, for a start. There may be commercial vested interests in urging this course now that private companies are increasingly involved in the running of prisons but all the evidence suggests that new prisons quickly fill up. A society that is spending its money on more prisons while closing hospitals and cutting spending on schools and universities has lost its way.

Identifying people who ought not to be sent to prison is another option. Many would argue that those who are mentally ill or have learning disabilities should not be in this type of custody and some argue that few, if any, women should be in prison. But the Government already claims to be committed to this and we haven't seen an end to overcrowding as a result.

A new approach

It's clear that we need a new approach to this problem. The size of the prison population depends, after all, not only on the number of people who are sent there but also the length of time they stay. And reducing the length of time an inmate stays is actually a much more reliable and efficient way of reducing the prison population than diversion or other approaches. That's not to say the other approaches should be dropped, but we should at least try both.

If all sentences were reduced by 10% the prison population would – quite quickly – decline by 10%. In England and Wales this would mean reducing the prison population from 85,000 to about 76,500, which would already make a massive difference to conditions and increase the scope for working usefully with prisoners. It's a perfectly feasible approach. All that is needed is political courage.

Consider a sentence of 20 months. This would be reduced to 18 months under the 10% proposal. Choosing the most appropriate length of a sentence is a matter of custom and practice – and it varies considerably between countries. No one could plausibly argue that 20 months is just right, but 18 won't do. Even for the most dangerous offenders, it seems odd to argue that the public is protected by detaining someone for ten years but safety would be jeopardised by releasing them after only nine. And does anyone think that a potential offender would be undeterred by four-and-a-half years, but would be stopped by the prospect of five?

There are other simple steps that could be taken as part of such a move, many of them imaginatively advanced by crime and justice academic Ken Pease years ago. Courts sentence in months and years and favour round figures (three months or six months seems for some reason to be preferable to four months and three weeks), but if they sentenced in days, terms could be readily reduced. Why not sentence someone to 150 days (if we like round numbers) rather than six months?

All these suggestions protect principles of proportionate justice, while deterrence and incapacitation would be unaffected. And rehabilitation would at last be given at least some opportunity to breathe and to thrive.

20 August 2014

⇨ The above information is reprinted with kind permission from *The Conversation*. Please visit www.theconversation.com for further information.

The death penalty

Every day, people are executed by the state as punishment for a variety of crimes – sometimes for acts that should not be criminalised. In some countries it can be for who you sleep with, in others it is reserved for acts of terror and murder.

Some countries execute people who were under 18 years old when the crime was committed, others use the death penalty against people who suffer mental problems. Before people die they are often imprisoned for years on 'death row'. Not knowing when their time is up, or whether they will see their families one last time.

The death penalty is cruel, inhuman and degrading. Amnesty opposes the death penalty at all times – regardless of who is accused, the crime, guilt or innocence or method of execution.

We have been working to end executions since 1977, when only 16 countries had abolished the death penalty in law or practice. Today, the number has risen to 140 – nearly two-thirds of countries around the world.

We know that, together, we can end the death penalty everywhere. Hafez Ibrahim was about to be executed in Yemen in 2007 when he sent a mobile text message to Amnesty. It was a message that saved his life. "I owe my life to Amnesty. Now I dedicate that life to campaigning against the death penalty."

The problem

Why the death penalty is wrong

Denial of human rights. Sentencing someone to death denies them the right to life – enshrined in the Universal Declaration of Human Rights.

Irreversible, and mistakes happen. Execution is the ultimate, irrevocable punishment: the risk of executing an innocent person can never be eliminated. Since 1973, for example, 150 US prisoners sent to death row have later been exonerated. Others have been executed despite serious doubts about their guilt.

Does not deter crime. Countries who execute commonly cite the death penalty as a way to deter people from committing crime. This claim has been repeatedly discredited, and there is no evidence that the death penalty is any more effective in reducing crime than imprisonment.

The death penalty is a symptom of a culture of violence, not a solution to it.

Often used within skewed justice systems. Some of the countries executing the most people have deeply unfair legal systems. The 'top' three executing countries – China, Iran and Iraq – have issued death sentences after unfair trials. Many death sentences are issued after 'confessions' that have been obtained through torture.

Discriminatory. You are more likely to be sentenced to death if you are poor or belong to a racial, ethnic or religious minority because of discrimination in the justice system. Also, poor and marginalised groups have less access to the legal resources needed to defend themselves.

Used as a political tool. The authorities in some countries, for example Iran and Sudan, use the death penalty to punish political opponents.

Amnesty is calling for

⇨ Countries who still use the death penalty immediately halt all executions.

⇨ Countries who have already stopped executing people, need to take this punishment off their legal books for all crimes, permanently.

⇨ All death sentences should be commuted to prison sentences.

Execution methods

There are many and varied types of execution used around the world today, including:

⇨ Beheading

⇨ Electrocution

⇨ Hanging

⇨ Lethal injection

⇨ Shooting in the back of the head and by firing squad

⇨ The above information is reprinted with kind permission from Amnesty International. Please visit www.amnesty.org.uk for further information and to read their annual review of the death penalty worldwide.

© Amnesty International 2015

KEY FACTS

101

As of July 2015, 101 countries have abolished the death penalty for all crimes.

22

In 2014, at least 22 countries around the world carried out executions.

2,466

In 2014, at least 2,466 people were sentenced to death worldwide – up 28% on 2013.

Support for the death penalty falls below 50% for first time

Findings from NatCen's *British Social Attitudes* today reveal that fewer than half of people in Britain back the death penalty – the first time support has dropped below 50% since NatCen began asking the public its view on capital punishment in 1986.

"Support for the death penalty stood at 74% in 1986, and then fell during the 1990s to 59% by 1998. The previous low of 52% was recorded in 2001"

NatCen's annual survey of the public's view on political and social issues shows only 48% of people now back the death penalty for "some crimes", down from 54% in 2013.

Support for the death penalty stood at 74% in 1986, and then fell during the 1990s to 59% by 1998. The previous low of 52% was recorded in 2001.

"The big change in public attitudes to the death penalty came in the 1990s at a time when attitudes to a range of other issues, like same-sex relationships and sex before marriage were also liberalising. This more recent change is interesting because attitudes have stayed fairly steady for a number of years"

Young people are consistently less likely to agree with the death penalty as older people. However, the difference is not that marked: 43% of 18–24s compared with 52% of those aged 65+ agree with the death penalty for some crimes. We also find big political differences on the issue, with UKIP voters far more likely to support the death penalty than the public as a whole (75% compared with 48%).

Rachel Ormston, Co-Head of Social Attitudes at NatCen Social Research said: "The big change in public attitudes to the death penalty came in the 1990s

at a time when attitudes to a range of other issues, like same-sex relationships and sex before marriage were also liberalising. This more recent change is interesting because attitudes have stayed fairly steady for a number of years. It could be the continuation of this liberalising trend or, perhaps, a response to the shocking botched executions in the United States that were widely reported in April and July of last year."

Notes

British Social Attitudes: the 32nd Report was published on 26 March 2015 and is freely available at: www.bsa.natcen.ac.uk.

Sample and approach – The 2014 survey consisted of 2,878 interviews with a representative, random sample of adults in Britain. Interviewing was mainly carried out between August and October 2014, with a small number of interviews taking place in November 2014. 2,376 people were asked about their views on the death penalty.

26 March 2015

⇨ The above information is reprinted with kind permission from *British Social Attitudes*. Please visit www.bsa.natcen.ac.uk for further information.

© *British Social Attitudes 2015*

Detecting crime using social media

'World-leading' predictive tools will be used by Met Police to monitor real-time crime events.

Researchers from the Social Data Science Lab have received research grants from the Centre for Scientific and Engineering Excellence at the Metropolitan Police Service and the ESRC Impact Acceleration Fund, to embed their world-leading and internationally recognised research on predictive analytics using social media into police operational processes.

The Lab Directors, Dr Matthew Williams from the School of Social Sciences and Dr Pete Burnap from the School of Computer Science & Informatics, have previously developed social media computational predictive models to estimate the emergence of disruptive crime events and the propagation of cyberhate.

Social media is generating high-volume data through multiple forms of online behaviour. Estimates put social media membership at approximately 2.5 billion non-unique users. The data produced by these users have been used to predict elections, movie revenues and even the epicentre of earthquakes.

Project lead Dr Burnap said: "Previous research that has examined the use of social media data in crime and policing contexts has been based in large metropolitan areas, such as Chicago and San Francisco. London, with its 2.5 million Twitter users, is the ideal city to further develop our social media and policing research using the COSMOS software platform. Social media data can be considered a form of open source intelligence that can assist the police in their real-time decision-making practices.

"These new grants will allow us to achieve a measurable impact within the Metropolitan Police Service, embedding our predictive social media models into their operational processes. MPS have kindly agreed to provide access to datasets that will allow us to validate our models against real-world crime incidents."

Dr Williams said: "There is a clear need in industry and the public and third sectors for a greater understanding of how these new forms of big social data can be marshalled to add value to existing practices. With the right statistical checks and balances in place and guided by criminological theory, social media data can complement and augment conventional police information to estimate crime patterns.

"The Social Data Science Lab is committed to generating world-leading research in the areas of crime, safety and wellbeing to inform a knowledge base that can be embedded in commercial, policy and practice domains."

A senior representative from the Metropolitan Police Service, said: "We have valued greatly our engagement with the Social Data Science Lab at Cardiff University to date as they have provided much needed insight into how social media can be exploited for the benefit of security and policing. They have already carried out some extensive research around identifying hate speech and the new project takes this further to develop and critique methodologies and tools for the identification of disruptive events and behaviour. We look forward to an innovative future with the Lab"

12 August 2015

⇨ The above information is reprinted with kind permission from Cardiff University. Please visit www.cardiff.ac.uk for further information.

Crime prevention lessons "essential" for protecting children from violent crimes, new report says

A new report has found that ten to 18-year-olds are more likely to be victims of crime than any other group, but only three in 20 violent crimes against children are reported, despite serious injuries.

The report by Victim Support and the University of Bedfordshire, *Suffering in Silence: Children and Unreported Crime*, was published today for the All Party Parliamentary Group for Victims and Witnesses of Crime.

The report finds that some young people perceive crimes including robbery, theft and assault as a "normal part of growing up" and many young victims do not report crimes. It also suggests that children and young people need to be given lessons in crime prevention and what to do if they are the victim of crime in the same way as they are taught about sex, alcohol and drugs.

Many children said they did not trust police so would not tell them if they were a victim of crime and others said they worried police would not believe them or would discriminate against them because of their age or race.

Some young people also believed reporting the crime would create further problems for them or have little faith that the police would even solve the crime. Instead, they would only tell a parent, teacher, carer or social worker about a crime if they had an established, trusting relationship with them.

The report recommends that teachers, social workers and medical staff get training to empower and support young crime victims appropriately, and for every school to have a commitment to keep their pupils safe.

Sarah Champion, MP for Rotherham and chair of the APPG for victims and witnesses of crime, said: "This research is a snapshot but confirms what I have been told on many occasions by children and young people. I am committed to looking more deeply into the questions this research raises to make sure children and young people get the support they need if they become the victim of a crime.

"Understanding crime, how to avoid becoming a victim and how to report it should be on the national curriculum just like education about sex, alcohol and drugs.

"But, care should be taken that the role police, teachers, medical staff and social workers play in supporting children and young people does not reinforce the fears they say they have about telling someone about a crime and so discourage them from telling anyone.

"It is only if they feel that they can go to the police that the perpetrators can be caught and punished – and hopefully future victims prevented."

Karen Froggatt, director, overseeing Victim Support's specialist work with child crime victims and witnesses, said: "Children and young people need to be given the confidence to talk to professionals – including the police – about what's happened to them. The police have to improve the way they treat children and young people. Other professionals must also be equipped to support young crime victims who, for whatever reason, feel they cannot go to the police.

"Our team sees first-hand the devastating impact a crime can have on children and young people. Regardless of whether they've gone to the police, we offer confidential advice and support. And, if they have to testify in court, our team is there to support them.

"As well as supporting children and young people directly, Victim Support shares its expertise by training staff in other organisations so that crime victims get the support they need and the respect they deserve."

Last year alone, the number of child victims of serious crime, abuse or neglect would fill 3,300 classrooms. Of those classrooms 950 would be filled by victims of sexual abuse. Victims of neglect would fill 2,400, victims of abduction would fill 20, and murdered children would fill at least two.

Victim Support has also been working on the development of a smart phone app with personalised instructions to help a young person escape immediate danger and on a new website which explains what it is like to be the victim of a range of crimes and what to do if they become a crime victim. These will be available in January 2015.

9 December 2014

⇨ The above information is reprinted with kind permission from Victim Support and the University of Bedfordshire. Please visit www.victimsupport.org.uk for further information.

Transforming lives: reducing women's imprisonment

The Prison Reform Trust has launched a three-year drive (2015–2018), supported by a major grant from the Big Lottery Fund, to reduce women's imprisonment across the UK. It will draw on the findings and recommendations of our report *Transforming Lives*, produced in partnership with Soroptimist UKPAC, and builds on the success of the previous programme supported by the Pilgrim Trust from 2012–2015, which contributed to a 10% reduction in the number of women in prison in England and Wales.

"Where women offend it usually turns out that at some stage they have suffered some type of addiction or abuse. We have failed to grasp that the problems of alcohol and drug dependency are widespread and the effects are wide reaching and expensive, with serious impacts on our society"

Sheriff, Scotland South

Too many women, many of whom are mothers, are sent to prison every year to serve short sentences for non-violent crimes, often for a first offence, a new Prison Reform Trust (PRT) briefing reveals.

The briefing marks the launch of a drive by the Prison Reform Trust, supported by a £1.2 million grant from the Big Lottery Fund, to reduce the number of women who are sent to prison for minor non-violent offences.

Last Thursday (23 July) the Justice Minister Caroline Dinenage reaffirmed the Government's commitment to reducing the number of women in prison in its response to the cross-party Justice Committee's report and recommendations on women offenders.

Two thirds of women sent to prison are mums and over 17,000 children are separated from their mothers by imprisonment every year. Imprisonment has a devastating impact on the life chances of these children, who as a result are more likely to experience homelessness, disruption to their family and home lives, problems at school and local authority care. Women released from custody are more likely to reoffend, and reoffend quicker, than women serving community sentences.

One woman former offender with an eight-year-old boy said:

"Once you come to prison you've got that hanging over you for the rest of your life... it's like a stigma. It follows you around. It's hard to get a job, a bank account when you can't prove the last three years of your history... little things like that. Having a criminal record is always going to affect your life."

The three-year UK-wide programme *Transforming Lives: reducing women's imprisonment* will promote more effective, early intervention and non-custodial responses to women in trouble, working with national and local governments, statutory agencies, and voluntary and community sector organisations in England, Wales, Scotland and Northern Ireland. The new programme will also have a base with Families Outside in Edinburgh, an independent charity working to support prisoners' families.

The briefing reveals that:

⇨ Eight in ten (81%) women entering prison under an immediate custodial sentence had committed non-violent offences.

⇨ Theft and handling offences are the biggest single driver to custody for women.

⇨ Women serving custodial sentences are twice as likely as men (21% v 10%) to have no previous convictions or cautions.

⇨ More than half (53%) of women in prison report having experienced emotional, physical or sexual abuse as a child, compared to 27% of men.

⇨ Women in prison are more than three times as likely to be identified as suffering from depression as women in the general population (65% v 19%).

⇨ In 2014, women accounted for 26% of all self-harm incidents in prison in England and Wales despite representing only 5% of the prison population.

⇨ Fewer than one in ten women leave custody with a job to go to, most face mounting debt and struggle to find safe housing.

PRT will identify and encourage the spread of good practice in working with women in contact with the criminal justice system, gathering and disseminating evidence to underpin innovation, and ensuring that the voices of often-marginalised women are heard in the corridors of power. PRT's work with the Soroptimists, reflected in the report *Transforming Lives*, provides a solid foundation for this three year programme.

Police diversion initiatives and cost-effective community sentences enable women to take control of their lives, care for their children and address the causes of their offending. Profiling the positive outcomes of these approaches will help to spread good practice and reduce the unnecessary and expensive use of remand and short custodial sentences.

There are opportunities to accelerate the pace of policy and practice change. Already in Scotland the decision to build a new women's prison has been reversed in favour of small custodial units and community-based provision.

In England and Wales, the new duty on the Secretary of State for Justice (in section 10 Offender Rehabilitation Act 2014) to identify and address the specific needs of women offenders should deliver better outcomes for women. In Northern Ireland a new step-down facility is being provided for women leaving prison.

Jenny Earle, director of the PRT's programme to reduce women's imprisonment, said:

"I am looking forward to working with partners across the UK to accelerate progress in reforming women's justice and reducing reliance on prison. We need to listen to women with experience of the justice system and take seriously the mounting evidence that short periods of imprisonment are particularly destructive for women and the families who rely on them."

Juliet Lyon, Director of the Prison Reform Trust, said:

"Most of the solutions to women's offending lie outside prison walls in treatment for addictions and mental health problems, protection from domestic violence, safer housing, debt management, education, skills

development and employment. The support of the Big Lottery Fund will enable us to lead a concerted drive to reduce the wasteful imprisonment of women and limit the devastating impact it has on the lives of their children and families."

Professor Nancy Loucks, Chief Executive of Families Outside, said:

"The impact on children when a family member goes to prison is significant and enduring, particularly when a mum goes to prison. Their housing may be at risk, their schooling may suffer, their care arrangements may mean they're separated from siblings and other family. Up to a third develop serious mental health issues, and they are at higher risk of offending themselves in later life."

Dawn Austwick, Chief Executive of the Big Lottery Fund, said:

"We are pleased to support the Prison Reform Trust to deliver this important work, looking at some complex and challenging social issues around reducing the number of women in prison. This UK-wide project builds on a strong body of independent evidence, looking at effective interventions to help women at risk of offending address underlying issues and improve their lives."

2015

"When a woman is processed through the criminal justice system, it is likely that those responsible for her case will not be from specialist domestic violence teams. All officers, not just those trained in domestic abuse, should be able to spot the signs and support women to disclose experiences of abuse. It is critical that police forces and the crown prosecution service work together to ensure that when they make decisions to charge women, enough has been done to identify potential links between domestic violence and their offence"

'Police fail to recognise that abuse often lies behind women's offending' the Guardian, 1 April, 2014

⇨ The above information is reprinted with kind permission from the Prison Reform Trust. Please visit www.prisonreformtrust.org.uk for further information.

© Prison Reform Trust 2015

Innovation hub will help police meet the challenges of modern day policing

Cutting edge technology and equipment that will help police meet the challenges of modern day policing are being developed in Sussex.

Assistant Chief Constable Steve Barry was at the opening of the Security Innovation and Demonstration Centre, part of the Home Office's Centre of Applied Science and Technology, at Langhurst, near Horsham, on Wednesday.

He said: "It's a privilege to give an end user perspective on what the centre can achieve. I'm particularly pleased that it is based in Sussex.

"The College of Policing, supported by the Police Digitisation Programme has committed to all forces being fully digital by 2016. A comprehensive review has already been undertaken, setting out a vision of what that looks like. Sussex, as well as all other forces is now fully behind making this happen.

"Cutting edge technology and equipment that will help police meet the challenges of modern day policing are being developed in Sussex"

"Technology is at the heart of seeing this vision through, allowing police officers to undertake their roles more effectively and at the same time making them more accountable to the public.

"Technology will allow us to provide digital evidence throughout the criminal justice system, maintaining the highest levels of quality and integrity. For example, Sussex Police is currently rolling out a mobile computing platform that will allow our response and neighbourhood teams to use mobile devices as they work to protect the community, enabling them to be more visible and spend less time in the office. Introducing mobile policing in Sussex is a major part of our plans to modernise how we work.

"It is not just existing solutions that are necessary if the police are to face the challenges of detecting and preventing crime that the 21st century brings. We need to produce new technical solutions to counter new types of crime and to deal with new forms of evidence. We also need solutions that can make our current processes more efficient or even bring about entirely new ways of working. This is a difficult challenge, but that doesn't mean impossible. We need to collaborate with both academic and commercial organisations to ensure we are fully equipped for the challenges ahead.

"With this in mind, we very much welcome initiatives like the Security Innovation and Demonstration Centre, which will support the continuation of the work we have already started."

The launch of the centre will showcase the UK's current and future policing capabilities in realistic environments, such as a neighbourhood policing scene and a serious crime scene, to demonstrate the benefits of various technologies in cutting crime and protecting the public.

SIDC, which began as a pilot project in May 2013, has so far supported the development of body-worn video (BWV), aiming to ensure that the technology is fit for police purpose, that it protects the privacy of others, and that the evidence collected is secure and admissible in court.

From January 2015, the centre will undertake a number of projects, which include:

⇨ Developing the 'digital police officer' – enabling officers to use technology such as BWV, wearable mobile data and head-up displays to improve information gathering and sharing

⇨ Supporting small businesses that are developing rapid drug and alcohol detection technology and improving explosive detection tools

⇨ Increasing understanding of how organised crime is taking advantage of an expanding digital world.

ACC Barry said: "Rather than each force working individually, through SIDC, forces, with a common goal, can work together to forge the partnerships necessary to bring about the rapid and transformational change required. Through SIDC, we can produce innovative solutions to the most pressing technical requirements in the most cost-effective way.

"Work has already started through SIDC to make body-worn video for use in a policing environment as effective as it can be. Initial work has begun to address the technical and policing challenges that need to be solved. Successful outcomes from this work will make the police more effective and more accountable, allowing us to serve the public efficiently and be trusted.

"I'm sure that the centre will have a huge role to play in the transformation of the criminal justice system to one that is digital by default and I look forward enormously to seeing that happen."

Commenting on the launch of the new Security Innovation and Demonstration Centre (SIDC) Police & Crime Commissioner, Katy Bourne, said: "I am extremely excited to see this national innovation hub open in Sussex. Innovation is at the heart of transforming public services, including policing.

"Modern policing is heavily dependent on new technology, which enables officers to provide a more effective and efficient service.

"Technology is also an essential part of ensuring the success of the UK in dealing with national threats and meeting the obligations under the Home Secretary's Strategic Policing Requirement is something that both the Chief Constable and I take very seriously.

"The SIDC will facilitate engagement between a wide range of suppliers, policy makers and end users to encourage collaborative partnerships. Specifically, this will enable the police and other emergency services to develop a better understanding of national security challenges and how technologies can be applied to help build capacity and capability to meet these requirements."

11 December 2014

⇨ The above information is reprinted with kind permission from Sussex Police. Please visit www.sussex.police.uk for further information.

Forecasting the time and place of crime hotspots

UCL researchers worked directly with police forces to spearhead the use of crime mapping and forecasting methods to prevent crime. In areas of implementation crimes such as burglary fell by 20–66%.

Over 35,000 cases of burglary are reported across England and Wales each month. Predicting where and when offences will occur has until recently proven very difficult. Combined with the erroneous belief that preventing crime in one location simply moves all of it elsewhere, this has led to a traditional police emphasis on detection. While detections are certainly important, as Benjamin Franklin noted, an ounce of prevention is worth a pound of cure.

Researchers at UCL Security and Crime Science have over the last decade developed tools that forecast the time and place at which crime is committed more accurately than was previously possible, and provides training in the use of these tools. Starting with the observation that crime hotspots are slippery, with many moving around over time, Professors Shane Johnson, Kate Bowers and Ken Pease demonstrated that the risk of burglary shows a pattern analogous to a contagious disease. Better prediction enables police officers to develop tactics that locate officers in the right place at the right time to prevent a crime from occurring.

Their research suggests that forecasting is possible because offenders often adopt 'foraging' strategies. They maximise benefits whilst reducing risk, for example by returning to houses they have already burgled, or to similar houses in the neighbourhood, for a matter of days or weeks, until they have exhausted the best opportunities or they begin to worry about detection by "going to the well once too often". Targeting crime prevention activity or police patrols in very small areas where a burglary has recently occurred can reduce the total number of burglaries. The techniques have wider applications, for example having been applied to forecasting the detonation of improvised explosive devices.

Training provided for, and engagement with, practitioners such as the police (by Professors Bowers, Johnson and Pease and Spencer Chainey), has led to the implementation of successful crime prevention strategies based on this approach. In 2010, Greater Manchester Police in Trafford (population 226,578) reduced burglary by using predictive maps to deploy police patrols and other resources to those areas expected to be most at risk. There was a 38% reduction in burglary over two years and the approach was extended to other crimes, achieving, for example, a 29% reduction in theft from motor vehicles.

It was an enormous but worthwhile effort to move this from the page to the reality of an operational setting. I'm very proud we developed a successful means for the mapping of future risk of crime, accompanied with a complementary system of police deployment. This was subsequently successfully adopted by a significant number of UK police forces. – Inspector Vincent Jones, Greater Manchester Police

Similar successes have been seen elsewhere in the country. In 2012 in North West Leeds (population 321,000), which had previously experienced the highest burglary rate in the country, a 48% decrease in burglary was accompanied by increased public confidence in the police. Similar approaches were used in Kent, West Mercia, and London. In Canada, a Neighbourhood Empowerment Team in the city of Edmonton developed an intervention based on the research, which reduced burglary by 66% in the trial area.

This has fed into policy at every level; researchers have served as expert witnesses to parliamentary select committees, advised Her Majesty's Inspectorate of Constabularies, and contributed to training courses provided by the College of Policing. The work has also received extensive media coverage through the BBC and the *New Scientist*.

16 December 2014

⇨ The above information is reprinted with kind permission from University College London. Please visit www.ucl.ac.uk for further information.

Governments increasingly resorting to the death penalty to combat crime and terrorism

⇨ States used the death penalty in a flawed attempt to tackle crime, terrorism and internal instability

⇨ Sharp spike in death sentences largely due to Egypt and Nigeria – at least 2,466 imposed globally, up 28% on 2013

⇨ 607 executions recorded, down almost 22% on 2013 (excluding those carried out in China, which executed more than the rest of the world put together)

⇨ 22 countries known to have executed, the same number as 2013

An alarming number of countries used the death penalty to tackle real or perceived threats to state security linked to terrorism, crime or internal instability in 2014, Amnesty International found in its annual review of the death penalty worldwide.

The number of death sentences recorded in 2014 jumped by almost 500 compared to 2013, mainly because of sharp spikes in Egypt and Nigeria, including mass sentencing in both countries in the context of internal conflict and political instability.

"Governments using the death penalty to tackle crime are deluding themselves. There is no evidence that shows the threat of execution is more of a deterrent to crime than any other punishment," said Salil Shetty, Amnesty International's Secretary General.

"The dark trend of governments using the death penalty in a futile attempt to tackle real or imaginary threats to state security and public safety was stark last year. It is shameful that so many states around the world are essentially playing with people's lives – putting people to death for 'terrorism' or to quell internal instability on the ill-conceived premise of deterrence."

But there was also good news to be found in 2014 – fewer executions were recorded compared to the year before and several countries took positive steps towards abolition of the death penalty.

Top executioners

China again carried out more executions than the rest of the world put together. Amnesty International believes thousands are executed and sentenced to death there every year, but with numbers kept a state

secret the true figure is impossible to determine.

The other countries making up the world's top five executioners in 2014 were Iran (289 officially announced and at least 454 more that were not acknowledged by the authorities), Saudi Arabia (at least 90), Iraq (at least 61) and the USA (35).

Excluding China, at least 607 executions were known to have been carried out in 2014, compared to 778 in 2013, a drop of more than 20 per cent.

Executions were recorded in 22 countries in 2014, the same number as the year before. This is a significant decrease from 20 years ago in 1995, when Amnesty International recorded executions in 42 countries, highlighting the clear global trend of states moving away from the death penalty.

"The numbers speak for themselves – the death penalty is becoming a thing of the past. The few countries that still execute need to take a serious look in the mirror and ask themselves if they want to continue to violate the right to life, or join the vast majority of countries that have abandoned this ultimate cruel and inhuman punishment," said Salil Shetty.

State security

The disturbing trend of states using the death penalty to combat threats against state security was visible around the world, with China, Pakistan, Iran and Iraq all executing people accused of 'terrorism'.

Pakistan resumed executions in the wake of the horrific Taliban attack on a Peshawar school. Seven people were executed in December, and the government has said it will put hundreds more convicted on 'terrorism'-related charges to death. Executions continued at a high rate in 2015.

In China authorities made use of the death penalty as a punitive tool in the

---

Reported executions in 2014

- Afghanistan (6)
- Belarus (3+)
- Egypt (15+)
- Equatorial Guinea (9)
- Iran (289+)
- Iraq (61+)
- Japan (3)
- Jordan (11)
- Malaysia (2+)
- North Korea (+)
- Pakistan (7)
- Palestine (State of) (2+, Hamas authorities, Gaza)
- Saudi Arabia (90+)
- Singapore (2)
- Somalia (14+)
- Sudan (23+)
- Taiwan (5)
- UAE (1),
- USA (35)
- Vietnam (3+)
- Yemen (22+)

Source: Death Sentences and Executions, 2014, *Amnesty International, first published 2015*

'Strike Hard' campaign against unrest in the Xinjiang Uighur Autonomous Region. Authorities executed at least 21 people during the year related to separate attacks, while three people were condemned to death in a mass sentencing rally conducted in a stadium in front of thousands of spectators.

"In a year when abhorrent summary executions by armed groups were branded on the global consciousness like never before, it is appalling that governments are themselves resorting to more executions in a knee-jerk reaction to combat terrorism and crime," said Salil Shetty.

In countries including North Korea, Iran and Saudi Arabia, governments continued to use the death penalty as a tool to suppress political dissent.

Other states made use of executions in similarly flawed attempts to tackle crimes rates. Jordan ended an eight-year moratorium in December, putting 11 murder convicts to death, with the government saying it was a move to end a surge in violent crime. In Indonesia, the government announced plans to execute mainly drug traffickers to tackle a public safety "national emergency" – promises it made good on in 2015.

Spike in death sentences

There was a dramatic rise in the number of death sentences recorded in 2014 compared to the previous year – at least 2,466 compared to 1,925 – a jump of more than a quarter. This was largely due to developments in Nigeria and Egypt, where hundreds of people were sentenced to death.

In Nigeria, 659 death sentences were recorded in 2014, a jump of more than 500 compared with the 2013 figure of 141. Military courts handed down mass death sentences against some 70 soldiers during the year in separate trials. They were convicted of mutiny in the context of the armed conflict with Boko Haram.

In Egypt, courts handed down at least 509 death sentences during 2014, 400 more than recorded during the previous year. This included mass death sentences against 37 people in April and 183 people in June following unfair mass trials.

Methods and crimes

Methods of executions in 2014 included beheading, hanging, lethal injection and shooting. Public executions were carried out in Iran and Saudi Arabia.

People faced the death penalty for a range of non-lethal crimes including robbery, drug-related crimes and economic offences. People were even sentenced to death for acts such as 'adultery', 'blasphemy' or 'sorcery', which should not be considered crimes at all. Many countries used vaguely worded political "crimes" to put real or perceived dissidents to death.

Regional breakdown

The Americas

The USA continued to be the only country to put people to death in the region, although executions dropped from 39 in 2013 to 35 in 2014 – reflecting a steady decline in the use of the death penalty in the country over the past years. Only seven states executed in 2014 (down from nine in 2013) with four – Texas, Missouri, Florida and Oklahoma – responsible for 89 per cent of all executions. The state of Washington imposed a moratorium on executions in February. The overall number of death sentences decreased from 95 in 2013 to 77 in 2014.

Asia Pacific

The Asia Pacific region saw a mixed bag of death penalty developments in 2014. Executions were recorded in nine countries, one fewer than the year before. Pakistan lifted a moratorium on execution of civilians. 32 executions were recorded in the region, although these numbers do not include China or North Korea, where it was impossible to confirm numbers. Indonesia announced plans to resume executions mainly of drug traffickers in 2015.

The Pacific continued to be the world's only virtually death penalty free zone, although the governments of both Papua New Guinea and Kiribati took steps to resume executions or introduce the death penalty.

Sub-Saharan Africa

Sub-Saharan Africa saw particular progress in 2014. 46 executions were recorded in three countries compared to 64 executions in five countries in 2013 – a drop of 28 per cent. Only three countries – Equatorial Guinea, Somalia and Sudan – were known to have carried out executions.

Madagascar took a progressive step towards abolition when the country's National Assembly adopted a bill abolishing the death penalty on 10 December, although the bill has to be signed by the country's President before becoming law.

Europe and Central Asia

Belarus – the only country in the region that executes – put at least three people to death during the year, ending a 24-month hiatus on executions. The executions were marked by secrecy, with family members and lawyers only being informed after the fact.

Middle East and North Africa

The widespread use of the death penalty in the Middle East and North Africa continued to be extremely troubling. Iran, Iraq and Saudi Arabia accounted for 90 per cent of all recorded executions in the region, and 72 per cent of all recorded executions globally (excluding China).

In 2014, executions were recorded in eight countries, two more than in 2013. 16 countries imposed death sentences – a large majority of countries in the region.

The overall number of executions recorded in the MENA region dropped from 638 in 2013 to 491 last year. These figures do not include hundreds of executions that are known to have occurred in Iran but which were not officially announced. In 2014, the Iranian authorities acknowledged 289 executions, however, reliable sources reported another 454 executions – bringing the total to 743.

31 March 2015

⇨ The above information is reprinted with kind permission from Amnesty International. Please visit www.amnesty.org for further information.

© Amnesty International 2015

Key facts

⇨ Latest figures from the Crime Survey for England and Wales (CSEW) showed that, for the offences it covers, there were an estimated 6.8 million incidents of crime against households and resident adults (aged 16 and over). This is a 7% decrease compared with the previous year's survey, and the lowest estimate since the CSEW began in 1981. (page 1)

⇨ Offences involving knives and sharp instruments increased by 2% in the year ending March 2015. This small rise masked more significant changes at offence level with an increase in assaults (up 13%, from 11,911 to 13,488) and a decrease in robberies (down 14%, from 11,927 to 10,270). In addition, the related category of weapon possession offences also rose by 10% (from 9,050 to 9,951). Such serious offences are not thought to be prone to changes in recording practice. (page 1)

⇨ While overall crime has fallen, vehicle-related offences have plummeted – there were 2,334 in the whole of 2014. It is the same in Suffolk, where vehicle crime fell from 7,152 to 3,186. (page 2)

⇨ There are two main ways crime is assessed in Britain –using figures provided by police forces and the Crime Survey for England and Wales (page 2)

⇨ Research is beginning to expose the high burden of mental illness faced by young people involved with gangs. Gang members are at increased risk of a range of mental health conditions including conduct disorder, antisocial personality disorder, anxiety, psychosis and drug and alcohol dependence. (page 4)

⇨ Knife crime has increased in England and Wales for the first time in four years, with the number of assaults with blades rising 13%, according to the latest set of police recorded crime figures. (page 5)

⇨ Home Office figures show that the number of police officers has fallen by a further 1,091 over the past year to 126,818. The number of operational frontline officers fell to 113,134 at the end of March, 12,000 fewer than in 2010 as a result of the austerity budget cuts. (page 5)

⇨ It is illegal to:

- sell a knife of any kind to anyone under 18 years old (16- to 18-year-olds in Scotland can buy cutlery and kitchen knives)

- carry a knife in public without good reason – unless it's a knife with a folding blade three inches long (7.62 cm) or less, e.g. a Swiss Army knife

- carry, buy or sell any type of banned knife

- use any knife in a threatening way (even a legal knife, such as a Swiss Army knife) (page 6)

⇨ Half of 11- 17-year-olds in the hands of Youth Offending Services have themselves been the victim of abuse, violence, crime or other traumatic experiences, finds a new report by Middlesex University. (page 7)

⇨ Constant access to the Internet and social media is creating new pressures and risks, with one in eight (12%) now reporting that they do not feel safe online. (page 8)

⇨ Evidence indicates that children and young people are at higher risk than adults of experiencing certain forms of crime. Females aged 16 to 19 years, for example, are the age group at highest risk of being a victim of a sexual offence. (page 9)

⇨ The majority of crimes against children and young people are not reported to the police. Only 13% of violent offences and 15% of thefts are reported by young victims. (page 9)

⇨ NSPCC/ChildLine have reported a 65% increase in contact from young people, adults and professionals regarding new technologies. Contacts recorded include a 168% increase in reports of online sexual abuse. Of those young people who have contacted NSPCC their experiences include:

- 12% cyber-stalking

- 12% unwanted sexual messages

- 8% asked to send or respond to a sexual message. (page 13)

⇨ In January 2015, the number of children in custody was 981. The first time on record the population has fallen below 1,000. Numbers have been falling steadily over the past decade, which is welcome, but it poses new and significant challenges for services. (page 16)

⇨ At age ten, children in England, Northern Ireland and Wales can be found guilty of a criminal offence. They can face trial and be placed in detention. (page 19)

⇨ On 23 May 2014, the prison population in England and Wales was 84,305 (page 20)

⇨ 101 people in this age group have died in prisons between 2007 and 2014. (page 26)

⇨ More than 15,000 assaults were committed by prisoners in 2013–14. (page 28)

⇨ NatCen's annual survey of the public's view on political and social issues shows only 48% of people now back the death penalty for "some crimes", down from 54% in 2013. (page 31)

⇨ In Nigeria, 659 death sentences were recorded in 2014. (page 39)

Age of criminal responsibility

The minimum age of criminal responsibility in England and Wales was set at ten in the 1963 Children and Young Person's Act. In the 1998 Crime and Disorder Act, Labour abolished the principle of *doli incapax*, whereby the prosecution had to prove that a child under 14 appearing in the criminal court knew and fully understood what he or she was doing was seriously wrong.

Crime

Crime may be defined as an act or omission prohibited or punished by law. A 'criminal offence' includes any infringement of the criminal law, from homicide to riding a bicycle without lights. What is classified as a crime is supposed to reflect the values of society and to reinforce those values. If an act is regarded as harmful to society or its citizens, it is often, but not always, classified as a criminal offence.

Custody

In criminal terminology, being 'in custody' refers to someone being held in spite of their wishes, either by the police while awaiting trial (remanded in custody), or, having received a custodial sentence, in prison or other secure accommodation. If someone has spent time on remand, that time is taken off their prison sentence.

Deterrent

Any threat or punishment which is seen to deter someone from a certain action: the threat of prison, for example, is expected to function as a deterrent to criminal behaviour.

Non-custodial sentence

A punishment which does not require someone convicted of a crime to be held in prison or another closed institution. Community sentences, restraining orders and fines are all types of non-custodial punishment.

Peer/youth court

An alternative approach to sentencing for young people. In the peer/youth court system, a young person who is charged with a crime appears in front of a jury of their peers for sentencing. The person being charged must agree to take part in the process.

Rehabilitation

The process by which an offender can learn, through therapy and education, to be a useful member of society on completing their sentence.

Reoffending rate

The rate at which offenders, having been convicted of a crime and punished, will then go on to commit another crime (implying that the punishment was ineffectual as a crime deterrent).

Restorative justice

This usually involves communication between an offender and their victim, family members, and possibly other people from the community or people affected by the crime. The purpose of the communication is to discuss the offending behaviour and come up with ways for the person to 'repay' the victim or community for their crime.

Sentence

The punishment given by a judge to a convicted offender at the end of a criminal trial. This generally takes the form of a fine, a community punishment, a discharge or a period of imprisonment.

Stalking

Repeatedly following, watching or harassing someone. Stalking usually takes place over a long period of time and is made up of lots of different actions, some of which may seem harmless but which can prove extremely distressing to the victim.

Assignments

Brainstorming

⇨ In small groups, discuss what you know about crime and justice in the UK. Consider the following points:

- What is the age of criminal responsibility in the UK?

- What is the Offender Rehabilitation Act?

- Have crime rates gone up or down in recent years?

Research

⇨ Research the law on carrying guns in the UK, the USA and one other country of your choice. Summarise your findings and include some details about the rate of gun-related crime in each country. You could also include graphs.

⇨ Choose a country where the death penalty is still in use and research Amnesty International's work in that country. Why does Amnesty International believe the death penalty should be banned? Write some notes and share with a classmate.

⇨ Choose a point from the *Youth Justice Timeline* on page 17 and do some more research. Write bullet points about your chosen point and share with the rest of your class.

⇨ Find out about a scheme in your local area that has been designed to help offenders, either while they are in prison or when they leave prison. Write some notes and feedback to the rest of your class.

Design

⇨ Design a poster or a series of online banners that will raise awareness of knife crime in the UK.

⇨ Choose one of the articles in this book and create an illustration to highlight the key themes/message of your chosen article.

⇨ Design a leaflet that explains how to peer/youth justice process works. Imagine that the leaflet will be given to a young offender who is trying to decide whether he/she wishes to go through the peer court system.

⇨ Design a website that will give young people information about what to do if they have been the victim of a crime.

⇨ Design an app that could be used to prevent crime.

Oral

⇨ Read the article *Half of young offenders are themselves victims, finds new study* on page seven. If you found out that a young offender was also a victim of crime, would it make you more sympathetic towards them? Discuss with a partner.

⇨ 'Social media has driven an increase in hate crime and should be banned.' Debate this statement a class, with half of you arguing in agreement and half of you against it.

⇨ As a class, re-enact a peer-justice led court case in which a 14-year-old boy punched another 14-year-old boy and broke his nose. Use the article on page 18 for information about how the process works.

⇨ Choose one of the illustrations from this book and, with a partner, discuss what you think the artist was trying to portray.

⇨ In pairs, recreate a 'restorative justice' scenario, in which the victim of a burglary meets the person who robbed them.

Reading/writing

⇨ Write an advice guide for young victims of crime, explaining how they can report a crime and what support they will receive afterwards.

⇨ Do you think films such as *Ocean's 11* or *Lock, Stock and Two Smoking Barrels* glamourise crime and criminal activity? What about video games such as the 'Grand Theft Auto' series? Give reasons for your answer.

⇨ Write a short story about someone drawn into a criminal lifestyle, and their attempt to rebuild their life following a spell in prison.

⇨ Watch the film 1994 *Shawshank Redemption*, starring Morgan Freeman and write a letter from the point of view of the character Brookes Hatlen explaining how he feels about life after being released from prison.

⇨ 'Ten-year-olds are not emotionally mature enough to be held criminally responsible for their actions.' Write 500 words exploring whether you agree or disagree with this statement.

⇨ Do you think the police in England should be able to carry guns? Write a blog post exploring your opinion.

Acknowledgements

The publisher is grateful for permission to reproduce the material in this book. While every care has been taken to trace and acknowledge copyright, the publisher tenders its apology for any accidental infringement or where copyright has proved untraceable. The publisher would be pleased to come to a suitable arrangement in any such case with the rightful owner.

Images

All images courtesy of iStock. Icon on page 41 courtesy of Freepik.

Illustrations

Don Hatcher: pages 3 & 21. Simon Kneebone: pages 18 & 35. Angelo Madrid: pages 7 & 31.

Additional acknowledgements

Editorial on behalf of Independence Educational Publishers by Cara Acred.

With thanks to the Independence team: Mary Chapman, Sandra Dennis, Christina Hughes, Jackie Staines and Jan Sunderland.

Cara Acred

Cambridge

January 2016